ROOT & BRANCH

BRITISH MAGIC

MÉLUSINE DRACO

& PAUL HARRISS

ROOT & BRANCH

First published in Great Britain by ignotus press 2002
BCM-Writer, London WC1N 3XX
© Melusine Draco & Paul Harriss

British Library Cataloguing in Publication Data
ISBN: 1 903768 05 5

Illustrator Doris Meyer
Edited by Claire Maguire
Printed in Great Britain by A2 Reprographics
Set in Baskerville Old Face 11pt

Table of Contents

ROOT & BRANCH

ntroduction

It is perhaps surprising to learn that only 35 species of tree are indigenous to the British Isles. The following are common native trees that a natural Witch should be able to recognise and utilise for magical purposes. Although strictly speaking the blackthorn and elder are classed as shrubs, their place as sacred or magical trees cannot be ignored and so their addition brings the number up to 37 of the most common that would have been familiar to the indigenous people of these islands.

The species covered in this book spread into the landscape naturally, that is, without the assistance of man. This was possible because about 10,000 years ago, at the end of the last Ice Age, there was still a land-bridge between Britain and the rest of Europe. About 7,000 years ago the 'British Isles' separated from the mainland as melting glaciers flooded what is now the North Sea and the English Channel. This natural barrier prevented the arrival of further species and so those that were already established here by that time are our own native species.

At that time, the British Isles was almost completely covered by trees – the natural Wildwood of our legends. When Neolithic man arrived around 4000BC, he began to clear the land for agricultural purposes and it is believed that by the late Roman period (AD400) man-made farm and moor-land had transformed the landscape. Although considerable amount of dense woodland remained, more was cleared in Anglo-Saxon and medieval times while other areas, many of which still exist, were turned into 'managed woodland' in the guise of royal hunting forests.

Not all the remaining woodland is ancient; nor are all woods that are not ancient, man-made. Left alone, Nature has a tendency to re-colonise almost any land in Britain that is allowed to remain idle. Open land is quickly invaded by trees such as birch and oak which readily colonise new territory.

Page 4

Throughout our long history, forests have been places of shelter, providing food for man and fodder for the animals; the wood for fuel (i.e. warmth and cooking) and for making weapons and other utensils.   At the same time they have also been places of fear, where the temperamental Faere Folk, wood sprites and elementals lurked in the dappled shadows.

Even today, few places can rival an English oak wood in early summer for peace and beauty with its carpet of primroses and blue-bells. Or the cathedral-like majesty of the autumn beech wood with the sun's light filtering through the leaves. Or the brooding quiet of the ancient holly wood. Perhaps it is not surprising that our remote ancestors performed their acts of worship in forest clearings and woodland glades for this was where they came face to face with 'Nature' - however they chose to see it.

What *is* hard to understand is the modern trend for many pagan practices to ignore many of our native trees and include introduced species into their tree-lore, despite the fact that they profess to be following the beliefs of the indigenous people of ancient Britain. This is, of course, understandable in the case of the strawberry tree, for example, which can only be found growing naturally in Ireland — but where is the alder and where is the beech? Why is ellen-wood often listed among the nine sacred woods suitable for the Beltaine-Fire when any seasoned countryman would tell you that it can never be burned without some risk to hearth or home?

So come and walk with us awhile into the Wildwood:

"Take my hand, child, and I will take you
safely through the Wild Wood."

Alder

The dampness of the English spring doesn't stop the common alder (*alnus glutinosa*), one of our most sacred of trees, from flowering during March and April. In fact, the trees are found growing by the waterside their little pink roots creeping into the water from the bank – some actually growing in the water. It is a tall, fine-leaved tree with crooked branches; the whole trunk bending towards the water and often hanging over it.

Alder woods, or 'carrs', are found all over the British Isles, even in the extreme north of Scotland, but only where the ground is water-logged. Alder woodland would have been more abundant when large tracts of the primeval forest comprised of undrained swamp especially in the mild, wet conditions that existed 10,000 years ago.

Since then, extensive drainage and clearance have reduced the carrs to their present fragmented state, often on the edge of fen or marsh common. In many areas alders are now only found along river banks or around small ponds; the presence of alder on dry ground is a sign of recent drainage or planting.

Bearing both catkins (male) and cones (female), the male catkins are greenish in colour and come before the leaves. The female catkins form in small clusters and resemble very small red-brown fir cones which appear in the autumn. The leaves of the alder are blunt with saw-like edges, and one half of the leaf is rarely the same size as the other. When young the leaves are sticky and shiny above, with a fine whitish down in the angles of the prominent veins underneath. The tree does not produce any seeds until it has passed its twentieth year.

The wood of the alder is soft and light in weight; the living wood being white. Once cut, however, it shows red and dries to a pinkish hue, which has earned it the name of Scottish Mahogany. Alder wood lasts a long time under water and was used by those who lived on the edges of the lakes, to make the piles on which their homes were built. For a more mundane purpose, the wood was turned into clogs because of its water-resistance.

In ancient times, the indigenous tribes of Britain regarded the tree as sacred, believing it to possess 'human' qualities when they first witnessed the white wood turning a vivid reddish-orange – the colour of blood. This caused the alder to be revered as a sentinel, guarding the realms of Otherworld. The tree was also sacred to incoming deities such as Eostre and Bran, the Celtic Raven god, while the Norsemen observed *'the lengthening month that wakes the alder and blooms the whin* (gorse) *'*, calling it *Lenct* – meaning Spring.

Originally it was one of the seven Celtic Chieftain trees but was displaced by the ash following the Battle of the Trees, which shows that it was sacred long before the Celts came to these islands. It is described as *'the very battle-witch of all woods, the tree that is hottest in the fight'* which suggests it may have been a military standard or clan totem belonging to the native people in their battles with the invading Celts.

The alder also has its associations with the Faere Folk, whom many believe to be the native people of the British Isles. The alder was used for its fine dyes: red from its bark, green from its flowers, brown from its twigs - with the green dye long being linked in British folklore with the green clothes of the Faere Folk.

Left to its own devices, thickets formed by the alder, usually together with a tangle of matted bramble and nettles, quickly become impenetrable to humans, yet provide an ideal habitat for the flora and

fauna of the water margin. This demonstration of the alder's continuing battle to reclaim the land which was lost to our native ancestors makes it an obvious candidate for the 'very prince of sacred trees'. Unfortunately, in modern Wicca and many areas of traditional Craft, the alder is sadly missing from their tree-lore.

Alder leaf

From a magical point of view it is unwise to attempt to fit the alder into any of the archetypal grouping popular with modern pagan belief. With the alder tree's habitat being streams and riverbanks it can be viewed as being sacred to Elemental Water, although with its various associations, it seems to embrace all four elements. Pipes and whistles were made from alder, making it sacred to Pan and Elemental Air; whistles can be used magically to conjure up destructive winds – especially from the North (Elemental Earth). Associated with the Elemental Fires of the smith-gods (because although it burns poorly, it makes one of the best charcoals) it has the powers of both dissolution and regeneration.

With its pale, flesh coloured timber turning blood-red when cut, the alder can also be seen in the symbolic terms of the Sacrificial God and embodying elemental Spirit and, with its Faere Folk associations, the gateway to Otherworld. Primarily, however, the alder is the tree of fire, using the power of fire to free the earth from water and a symbol of resurrection, as its blooms heralds the drying up of the winter floods by the Spring Sun.

The indigenous people would have used the 'natural' calendar to calculate the re-emergence of the sun and so alder is ideal to use as an integral part of the celebrations for Spring Equinox. Just as the tree itself can be seen as the embodiment of all the elements, so its use can bestow both negative and positive outcomes to any magical working.

Great care needs to be taken when working with alder-power since there is an unpredictability surrounding it – as one would

Alder cones

expect with anything associated with the Faere Folk. When collecting flowers, cones, leaves or wood it is advisable to leave something in exchange for what you take. Used as incense, alder can be used to disperse other powers and to dissolve malevolent forces. On the other hand, when burnt it can also cause dissention between even the closest of relationships — and the felling of a sacred alder will be revenged by fire in the home.

Hang a sprig in your home, however, and alder brings you and yours under the protection of powerful forces, which will both attract good fortune and banish negative powers. Collect this before the Autumnal Equinox when both cones and catkins are fully developed. The dried cones also make suitable decorations to add to Yuletide gifts or as spicy pot pourri.

Perhaps it is this unpredictability that makes modern pagans shy away from working with alder-power since the tree is neither benign nor benevolent. For serious magical practitioners, however, the uncertainty of working with the alder is part of its irresistible challenge as a 'battle-witch' which all its connotations of ancient ancestral power.

Staff or Wand

A staff or wand cut from the alder should be obtained with great care. Since this is a tree under the protection of the Faere Folk, a libation of milk or fruit, and the offering of a small silver coin would be appropriate. Do not underestimate the power of the alder as the combination of all the elemental symbols makes it a formidable wand or staff to wield. Once you have found your tree and agreed a 'price' make sure you take it with a swift, clean cut. Prepare the wood in the normal way but do not allow others to handle it, particularly if used as a staff or stang.

Ash

The common ash (*fraxinus excelsoir*) is native to Britain and most of Europe, being widespread throughout the country in oak woods, copses, in hedgerows and along river banks. Recognising the ash is easy because the twigs in winter and the foliage in summer are so distinctive. In the spring the silvery grey twigs show characteristic velvety black buds; the leaves are formed in 3-6 pairs of toothed, lance-shaped arrangements. The ash is one of the latest trees to come into leaf which gives rise to the country rhyme which associates it with Elemental Water.

> *Oak before ash, we're in for a splash;*
> *Ash before oak, we're in for a soak!*

The ash loses its leaves quite early in autumn and are frequently shed at the first hint of frost, although the bunches of ash keys last well into the winter to provide food for the birds. The name of ash 'keys' dates from medieval times when door keys were fashioned in the shape of the seed pods of the ash tree.

Ash has always been highly prized for firewood because it burns 'green', that is unlike many other woods, it is suitable for hearth fires when it has been freshly cut. Another advantage of ash timber is that it is so tough and elastic that it can withstand stress, strain and sharp knocks and so throughout history it has been used for tools and weaponry, especially for the shafts of spears and lances. The Anglo-Saxon word for ash is *aesc*, which was also used to mean spear.

From very ancient times, the ash has been revered as a sacred and fortunate tree, connected with fire, lightning and clouds. In some pagan mythologies it appears as an ancestor of mankind, although it appears to have displaced the alder when in-coming tribes defeated the indigenous people of Britain.

The ash played an important role in ancient Nordic mythology where it was regarded as the 'tree of life'. From a huge ash tree, whose crown reached up to heaven and whose roots penetrated down into Otherworld, the gods ruled the world. To watch over earthly affairs, they were helped by an eagle perching on the top-most branches; the eagle was assisted by a squirrel, which spent its time scampering up and down the tree taking messages.

Because of its sacred and magical character, the ash was some-times considered a dangerous tree to cut down without the necessary propitiatory observances. As late as the 18th and early 19th centuries, Derbyshire people still believe that anyone wantonly destroying an ash tree would certainly be deported as a result of misfortune.

Unlike the alder with its Faere Folk associations, the ash is benevolent and friendly to mankind. It cured diseases; it could be used in divination and charms. Its leaves and wood protected all who kept them in the house or wore them, from all sorts of evil – in later times they were used as a charm against Witchcraft! The dividing line between magic and medicine can become blurred when referring to old remedies but both would have been the province of the local wise or cunning women.

In Lincolnshire, the berried, female ash was known locally as 'sheder' and used to defeat the spells of male Witches, while the berry-less variety, or 'heder' was used against female Witches. This indicates that the charm was an old charm against evil long before it was hijacked by the christians.

In Devonshire, new-born babies are given their first bath by a fire of ash-wood. Probably the best known ash-cures is that used in the treat-ment of ruptures and rickets in children. The rites differ from county to county but there are records of this effecting a cure.

Willow bark helps to reduce high fevers and

to relieve the pain of arthritis and headaches. Although these claims have not been proven clinically, the indications are strongly supported by the fact that the bark was used in a similar way to aspirin long before the invention of the drug.

The leaves of the ash have been used to treat all manner of complaints. Dried they can be taken as a gentle form of laxative, to ease colic, help pass kidney stones and as a treatment for gout, rheumatism, jaundice and flatulence. An infusion of ash leaves in the bath is said to soften the skin.

Magically the leaves can be used in any rites of regeneration—either in incense or as part of your cleansing bath. They are particularly powerful when used in negative magic or charms for protection—either as incense or carried in a charm bag, which works just as well for people, animals or the family car.

Ash keys can be taken as a brew to help bridge the void between the worlds; as an aid to divination or scrying; or in a spell for prosperity – particularly if burned at the Winter Solstice.

The wood is used as a charm to protect against vampires (psychic or otherwise) and is known to contain mild treatment against malaria and fever.

Although in modern British Wicca the ash is often referred to as 'the Goddess tree', and associated with the Triple Goddess, this is rather misleading and quite inaccurate. In classical Norse, Greek and Celtic literature, the ash is seen to have predominantly *masculine* associations. From natural history's point of view, the ash can undergo a sex change from year to year; a male tree of last year may be female this year, and perhaps bisexual the next.

This means that the tree is the perfect magical androgyny – i.e. its sexual/magical/mystical propensities are interchangeable and that it can be 'both, either or neither' as symbolised by Kether in Qabalistic terms.

The ash is one of the 'Nine Woods of the Beltaine Fire' - the others being birch, yew, hazel, rowan, willow, pine and thorn and

Ash leaves, buds and keys

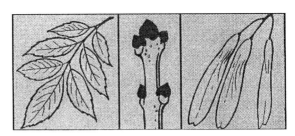

one of the Irish 'Chieftain Trees'. The availability of the individual woods will, of course, differ in different parts of the country, so any of the other trees mentioned as being part of our traditional heritage may be used, with the exception of oak. Traditional craft-lore simply states that the fire should consist of nine woods with the exception of oak.

The traditional ash-faggot is made up of ash twigs and burned at Yule to ensure good fortune in the coming year. This is the origin of the Yule log and a miniature one can be kept in the house for good luck.

Staff or Wand

According to country-lore, snakes cannot stand ash and will keep well away from anyone carrying a staff made from it despite the fact that it is the tree of Mercury, whose symbol is the caduceus. All deities associated with the ash appear to have a penchant for magical illusion and so an ash wand would be useful when used for glamouring or enchantment. In Traditional Craft, both the coven or personal stang or staff was cut from an ash tree as this represents the Horned God. Dressed with garlands and with crossed arrows, the staff was used as an altar, although a personal staff should be left plain.

According to Evan John Jones (*Witchcraft – A Tradition Renewed*), "When an ash staff is found, you will know it is the one for you. It will feel right to the hand. A slight tingling in the fingers will tell you that it is yours and yours alone ... When taking the staff, a small coin is left behind as payment."

Aspen

One of the most hauntingly beautiful of our native trees, the aspen (*populus tremula*) is also one of our less familiar. Sometimes referred to as the 'quaking aspen' or 'shiver-tree' because its leaves tremble in the slightest breeze, the tree has been the source of much folk-lore, all associating this lovely tree with evil and gossip.

The aspen is a species of fast-growing poplars which can quickly reach a height of 65ft. It is more common in the north where they are most often seen on hillsides and valleys, especially where the soil is fairly damp and light. It does, however, grow in hedgerows and copses, and is quite often seen in open oak-woods.

The aspen flowers in March before the leaves appear, bearing separate male and female catkins on separate trees. The catkins produce no scent or nectar, so they are not visited by any pollinating insects; pollination is carried out by the wind.

The shape and size of the leaves vary according to whether they come from the main part of the tree or from the suckers. The leaves are copper-brown when they first break, turning to grey-green — usually paler on the underside which gives the aspen its curious shimmering silver light. In the late autumn the leaves turn to gold in a spectacular display. The leaves turn inwards, and one country superstition says that the leaves curl upwards when a thunderstorm is due.

Timber from the aspen is very light and not particularly durable but it is often used for veneer and plywood, for matches and light boxes for fruit and vegetables. Today it is widely used for pulp and paper, while in the past, it was turned into arrows. In Scotland aspen wood is little used because of the trees folk-lore. Geoffrey Grigson, writing in *The Englishman's Flora* comments rather cynically: "If the timber had been tougher, harder, more durable, and more valuable, perhaps the legends would have been different."

If the aspen has little commercial worth, it has been much admired by artists and poets. Gerard Manley Hopkins wrote some famous lines in memory of the aspens at Binsey near Oxford after they had been cut down:

> *My aspens dear, whose airy rages quelled,*
> *Quelled or quenched in leaves the leaping sun,*
> *All felled, felled, all are felled.*

The aspen's 'airy rages' have been the source of much local folk-lore and legends—although most have a biblical basis. This usually means that a tree or plant originally had 'pagan' associations and so we need to look much deeper behind the latter-day christian superstitions. For the aspen to receive such 'bad press', it must have figured largely in pre-christain beliefs, as did the elder (or ellen-tree) which suffered the same fate in being labelled the tree from which Judas hanged himself (see page 42).

The constant movement and rustling of the leaves has also led to the connections with the sound of gossip and loose tongues. This is recorded in Scotland, where the tree is known as 'old wives' tongues'. In parts of Berkshire it is referred to as 'women's tongue' and the Welsh name for the aspen *coed tafod merched*, also conjures up the same image; as does the Manx name, *chengey ny mraane*.

In Witch-lore, no tree is looked upon as being 'evil' although each species may have different propensities for averting negative energies. It may be worth tracing the aspen's names in Anglo-Saxon (*Aespe*) and Old Irish (*Eadha*) to see if there are any references to the part it played in pre-christian folk-lore. Considering the aspen is one of our indigenous trees, it would be extremely rare to find little or no mention of it in the old oral traditions, especially as it had some recorded healing powers.

On the plus side, the aspen is credited with the power to cure agues and fevers. A very old sympathetic magical charm held that ailments could be treated by something that resembled their effects or symptoms — and since ague causes the patient to shake and tremble, s/he was more likely to be healed by the shaking tree.

In *Folklore of the Northern Counties* (1879), William Henderson records the Lincolnshire belief that to be cured of the ague the sufferer should pin a lock of their hair to the tree and say: *"Aspen-tree, aspen-tree, I prithee to shake and shiver instead of me."* As is usual in many healing charms, the journey home must be made in complete silence, otherwise the magic will be negated.

Another method is to bore a small hole in the bark and insert the patient's nail-parings; the hole is then closed up and once the bark has grown over the opening, so the affliction will disappear.

Much of our native wood-lore has been submerged under a thin veneer of modern paganism but for our ancestors, these indigenous trees were the focal point of the spiritual nature of these very Islands. In the wilder, remote places there is still the belief that the 'little' or 'fair people' of the *sidh* (Irish) or *y twlwyth teg* (Welsh) can be contacted via certain trees which must be respected at all costs, otherwise harm will befall those who adopt a cavalier attitude to such sacred places.

From the magical perspective, the aspen is seen at its best on a moonlit summer night; when warm breezes stir the leaves it is possible to believe that this is another tree that might once have been associated with the Faere Folk.

The fact that the tree is pollinated by the wind; that its wood was used for arrows, plus the constant movement of the leaves all point to the aspen being associated with Elemental Air. Despite its size, it is a short-lived tree and so symbolises the transience of this earthly existence. It this capacity it can be used as part of Otherworld rituals and funerary rites of passage either included in the incense mix or as garlands.

Aspen leaves, buds and catkins

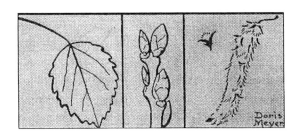

Since its traditional use was in the production of arrows, it may also be appropriate to fashion the pair that normally decorate the coven stang (see page 13) out of aspen wood. The symbol of the arrow is another connection to the Faere Folk as they were a dab hand at archery.

Much of what is written here is, of course, pure conjecture but for those who still possess the spirit of adventure, re-establishing a working relationship with the aspen might just produce some interesting results.

Staff or Wand

Because timber from the aspen is not of particularly good quality, it will take a lot of patience and hard work to produce a magical tool and even then, it will not be very robust. For this reason, it would probably be inadvisable to cut a staff from aspen since this would not be strong enough to stand up to rigorous circle work as a staff or stang. The otherworldliness of the tree would also make it suitable as a funerary wand, if such a tool was to be interred or cremated with a respected member of the coven or group. When selecting a small branch for your wand make sure you leave a suitable offering that symbolises air, such as food for the birds.

Beech

Although the common beech (*fagus sylvatica*) is classed as one of the native trees of the British Isles, pollen records show that it only arrived some 3,000 years ago compared with other species. There are, for example, many early records of alder wood and catkins dating back 10,500-9,500 years from Yorkshire, while the ash was known to be present in southern and central England between 7,000-6,000 years ago.

Current pollen data reveals the differences in origin, directions of spread and timing of the spread for each individual species which indicate that the beech arrived from the south-east much later and explains why the beech is not represented in the tree-alphabet as the latter pre-dates the time when the beech became wide spread in Britain.

The fact that Julius Caesar recorded 'there are no beech trees in Britain' strengthened the belief that this magnificent tree arrived with the Romans. This is now known from the pollen records to be incorrect but the tree was certainly a British rarity in Roman times, although it is now the third most common tree in British woodlands.

A mature beech tree is an impressive sight at any time of the year with its smooth grey bark and distinctive foliage. In the spring the new leaves fringed with soft silvery hairs have a shining, translucent appearance; turning dark and glossy as summer approaches. The flowers are followed by the nuts, developing inside a bristly case. In October the cases burst open to allow the 'beech-mast' to fall out, so that the delicious nuts can be gathered and eaten.

Woodland animals such as badgers and squirrels are particularly fond of beech nuts and for birds such as nuthatches and bramblings a plentiful supply can increase their changes of surviving a bad winter. A really heavy crop occurs about every four or five years and in the past it was common for pigs to be turned out into the woodlands to forage about for nuts and acorns. This common grazing still occurs in parts of the New Forest and is called 'pannage'.

In autumn the beech really comes into its own with the leaves turning from orange, russet and gold until they fall to the ground in a thick carpet of dull copper. Because of the dense foliage there is little that will grow in the shade of a beech tree and so the tree casts a large golden circle on the woodland floor. Younger trees and beech hedges often keep their leaves until the following spring when the winter twigs with their spear-shaped buds wait to burst into life again.

Despite their massive trunks, beech trees are shallow rooted, which makes them susceptible to storm damage. If they survive, and beeches will reach 100 ft when fully grown, the beech's normal life span is about 300 years—although some of the ancient pollards at Burnham Beeches are known to be over 400 years old. Other 'hulks' at Windsor Forest and Wyre Forest may be even older. Pollarded trees eventually become hollow and this enables them to live for centuries since they are much better equipped to stand up to strong winds.

In his book, *Ancient Woodlands*, Oliver Rackham points out that "the ecology is perhaps better known than of any other native tree. In southern England, it has been a valuable timber since the

Bronze Age". Despite the magnificence of the beech, there is surprisingly little in terms of British folk-lore associated with the tree, apart from it offering protection from lightning. In terms of European history, the only records of it having any cultural significance are pre-historic in that the beech appears to have been of great importance to certain Iron Age Celtic groups from Central Europe.

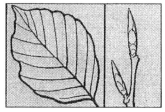

Beech leaves and buds

Beech wood is white, or even reddish if it is grown on very rich soils—and very heavy when newly felled. It is close-grained, hard and smooth, being one of the strongest of native timbers. According to the celebrated poet and countryman, Geoffrey Grigson, the wood 'endures best under water or in waterlogged soil' and to support this claim, the piles under Winchester Cathedral and some of those under the old Waterloo Bridge were made of beech. Other sources, however, state that the timber's use is limited because it decays quickly.

On a more domestic front, it is a very good wood for kitchen utensils, furniture making and sports equipment. It burns well and is used in Scotland to smoke herrings—while the charcoal made from beech 'is well suited for the manufacture of gunpowder'. Queen Victoria is said to have preferred to burn beech wood from Burnham Beeches on the fires at Windsor Castle.

Beech trees *'make spreading trees, and noble shades with their well-furnished and glittering leaves ... the shade, unpropitious to corn and grass, but sweet and of all the rest most refreshing to the weary shepherd.'* John Evelyn, 1729.

In *The White Goddess*, the notes suggest that the Franks and Achaeans originally consulted beech oracles but, finding no beeches on their migrations, transferred their allegiance to the oak, its nearest equivalent, to which they gave the name *phegos* — the same word as *fagus*, the Latin for beech.

Beech is also a common synonym for literature, with the English word 'book' being etymologically connected with the word

Beech mast still in its case

'beech' from which writing tablets were made. Venantius Fortuna-tus, the 6th century bishop-poet wrote: *Barbara fraxineis pingatur runa tabellis*, "Let the barbarian rune be marked on beechwood tablets". Magically, therefore, we can associate the tree with know-ledge and learning.

The beech has always been recognised for a number of medicinal properties, with Culpeper recommending beech leaves as a cooling agent to alleviate swellings by boiling them to make a poultice. In Europe, beech nuts were eaten in times of famine and in France, the nuts are still sometimes roasted to provide a coffee substitute. The nut oil can also be used for cooking.

Staff or Wand

It is rare for beech wood to be used as a staff or wand but it is by no means taboo simply because the tree was omitted from the tree-alphabet. As the tree has connections with knowledge and learning, it makes it an obvious choice for those who pursue their magical quest on a more intellectual level. To obtain a staff of a suitable thickness may prove to be difficult, however, since the branches of the required thickness may well be out of reach.

It is interesting to note that while the beech is often described as the 'queen of the woods', those who work with beech staffs and wands maintain that the energies from this tree are most definitely male and aligned with Element Earth. Therefore the offering or libation would need to be something decidedly masculine – such as vintage port.

Birch

There are two native birches, the downy birch (*betula pubescens*) and the silver birch (*betula pendula*). (There is a third dwarf shrub (*betula nana*) which can be found in northern England and Scotland). This was one of the earliest trees to colonise Britain after the last ice age with pollen records having been found that date back to 13,500 years, although it is believed to have become very rare or even on the verge of extinction between 11,000 and 10,200 years ago.

With its characteristic silvery bark and delicate leaves it is easy to appreciate why the birch has inspired painters, poets and writers down through the centuries. For example:

'Beneath you birch with silver bark,
And boughs so pendulous and fair,
The brook falls scattered down the rock;
And all is mossy there.'
Samuel Taylor Coleridge

Known as 'the Lady of the Woods' the birch is a tree of Venus and therefore associated with Elemental Water.

The silver and downy birch are very similar. The silver birch, as its name suggests, has a paler, silvery bark; the downy birch has a bark that is more variable in colour from silver-grey to brown. One way of telling the difference is by the areas of black, knotted bark on the lower part of the trunk of the silver birch with its 'weeping' twigs. The downy birch is smooth right down to the ground and its twigs point upwards.

The small leaves appear towards the end of April and after a heavy shower it is possible to detect a delicate fragrance from the aromatic resin that is washed from the unfurling leaves and twigs. In the autumn the leaves turn bright yellow before falling, leaving the bare trees gleaming in the winter sunlight.

Birch trees appear to attract a large number of birds' nests among the branches but these are, in fact, galls — a natural deformity known as a 'witches broom'. A name that also derives from the cutting of birch twigs to make the traditional witches' broom or besom. Large amounts of birch brushwood are used to fill out the jumps at racecourses during the National Hunt season.

Birch timber is a pale, creamy colour and although it is a hard wood, its uses tend to be more domestic than outdoors.

Both species produce a bitter, astringent, tonic that has diuretic and mild laxative effects; it reduces inflammation, relieves pain and increases perspiration. This can be used internally for rheumatism, arthritis, gout, water retention, cystitis, kidney stones, skin eruptions and fevers. Externally, it is used mainly in the form of birch tar oil, for the treatment of psoriasis and eczema. The sap can also be fermented to make beer, wine, spirits or vinegar and Culpeper recommends it 'to break the stone in the kidneys and bladder', and as a mouthwash.

The folk-lore associated with the birch is wide and varied since it can be used as a protective charm against evil spirits, bad luck and the evil eye—or for a spell for fertility and love.

The birch is another of the 'Nine Woods of the Beltaine Fire' and makes excellent kindling for camp fires as the wood burns well. Birch kindling was used to set alight the ritual fire at the rising of the first sun in May to herald the approach of the warmer weather. The tree was also believed to have life-giving properties and in some parts of the country, birch branches were hung over the doors on Midsummer Eve as they were considered to be symbols of return and renewal.

Many different areas have their own version of 'beating the boundaries' which is traditionally carried out to remind a particular community where their territory officially ended. This was a symbolic and magical casting of a protective 'circle' against the dangers from outside and to cast out all negative energies from within the boundaries.

To make use of the trees protective energies, collect a handful of thin birch rods and fashion them into a long broom-head. Circle the boundary of your home and garden (or land), sweeping all the 'dirt' (and unclean spirits) outwards away from the home, beating the ground and significant boundary markers such as fence posts where it is necessary to change direction, or where there are gateways, etc.

The birch was also associated with corrective powers and in medieval times, a bundle of birch rods was carried in front of the magistrate on his way to court, both as a symbol of his authority and as a means of correction. Birch rods were used to beat felons (and sometimes the mentally ill) to rid them of the demons causing their affliction and was still used as a punishment in the Isle of Man until recently.

On a much gentler note, birch is supposed to be feminine and lucky, as the tree of birth and rebirth. Strips of birch bark can be used as a magical writing surface, particular for love spells, while the wood can be used as incense connected with romance. The birch is also used as garlands to decorate the ritual area, especially at spring and summer celebrations.

It is said that birch trees were often used as the May Pole, erected every year at the Beltaine festival and then kept in the stable or farm yard afterwards to protect the household and livestock and especially horses from being 'hag-ridden', although this is difficult to verify with any degree of certainty.

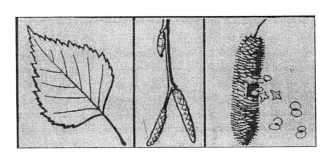

Birch leaf, buds and catkins

Staff or Wand

This is a sacred shamanic tree and so practitioners should carry a birch wand or staff to aid their journeys in this world and through the astral planes. The place of the birch staff within magical rites is that of the bridge between the worlds.

The handle of the witches' broom is, of course, a form of staff, cunningly concealed as a simple domestic implement, although this is the *male* component of the besom, often with a phallic shaping to the handle at one end, it is fashioned from alder, ash or birch. The actual brush part of the besom is symbolic of the female component which is made up of certain twigs, including the birch, hazel and broom.

As can be seen, there are so many different facets to the birch tree that it would be a mistake to attempt to pigeon-hole its energies merely for convenience sake or to fit in with any preconceived ideas about tree magic. A light wine would make an ideal offering in payment for your wand or staff, especially if the wine had been made from birch sap.

Blackthorn

The blackthorn (*prunus spinosa*) is probably the tree (or more correctly, shrub) most strongly identified with traditional British Old Craft through its long associations with magic and the Faere Folk. Mentioned in Celtic Brehon law, it is even supposed to have its own special tribe of Faere guardians who will take revenge on anyone cutting a branch from the tree at either the old opening or closing of the year.

Archaeological research has established that the fruit from the blackthorn — sloes — which were common in the wild, were consumed in large quantities as far back as Neolithic times. These ancient references probably explain the deep rooted fear of the blackthorn as something that is best avoided since it represents the displaced, indigenous people of these islands. In later times, the Faere Folk and witches were said to be one and the same.

The blackthorn is a deciduous shrub, common throughout the British Isles. It does grow in woodland but because it needs plenty of light, it is unlikely to be found under dense cover, preferring the edges of woods, clearings, along road verges, grassy tracks, hedgerows, embankments and on commons. This is a rigid bush with a tangle of vicious spikes that offer nesting birds a large degree of protection from predators.

The blackthorn hedge

The bark is usually black — hence its name — and in the spring the blackthorn breaks into a mass of pure white blossom. The shrub flowers early, in March or April, before the leaves appear. In some years the profusion of white starry blossom completely obscures the bark. There is an old country saying that if the weather is cold when the blackthorn flowers then it will remain cold for the whole flowering period — about a fortnight — a so-called 'Blackthorn Winter'.

The small leaves unfurl in May to complete an almost impenetrable hedge or thicket, especially in cold, exposed, or coastal area. The flowers are succeeded by hard green fruits which ripen during the summer to become the familiar blue/black sloes, each one coated with a natural dusty bloom. If these are left on the bush until late autumn they do become sweeter and can be used to produce sloe-gin, a delightful liqueur.

The blackthorn sends up erect shoots or suckers from its roots and if these are not cut back they gradually spread to form a dense thicket which is extremely difficult to remove. In a short time a large stand of blackthorn can result from just one parent plant. This method of re-colonising, and its Faere Folk connections make an ideal symbol for Elemental Earth.

Blackthorn wood is hard and the grain forms intricate patterns of colour. Ireland's fearsome cudgel, the shillelagh, is cut from the main stem of the blackthorn, while the straight stems from younger bushes make handsome walking sticks or staffs.

Another country tradition involves the weaving of a garland or 'crown' from the thin twigs of the blackthorn to be used as a Yuletide decoration. The garland was burned on New Year's Day and the ashes scattered on the fields to ensure a good crop, both in terms of agriculture and livestock, in the coming year.

From medieval times the tree's medicinal purposes have been recorded: blackthorn flowers were used as a tonic and mild laxative; the leaves as a mouthwash and to stimulate the appetite; the bark to reduce fever; the fruit for bladder, kidney and digestive

disorders. According to medieval herbalists, the shrub was held to be 'the regulator of the stomach' since its flowers loosened the bowels and its fruit bound them. The bitter fruit of the blackthorn was made into jellies, syrups, jams, wine and *verjuice* (an acid liquor). Sloes were also used to make sloe gin and were an ingredient in fruit cheeses.

Sloes can also be used for wart charming and the following is still in use in some parts of the country. Rub a wart with a plump, juicy fruit and then dispose of it. Before the sloe has dried out, the wart will have vanished. Alternatively, rub each wart with a scrap of meat and hang the meat on a thorn for the same result.

Because of its cultural links with the Faere Folk, the blackthorn is known as the 'Faere Wishing Bush'. Collect a flower or leaf and put it in a charm bag with your special wish written on parchment. Alternatively, fasten a scrap of ribbon or fabric to one of the thorns as you make your wish. The spikes from the blackthorn have long been used to pierce wax images, both for cursing and healing purposes.

The wood and dried berries can be used as incense in rituals of banishing negativity and so it is as well to collect a small supply of these to dry out and use in a special blend of your own, as and when necessary. Anoint a few twigs of blackthorn with oil and burn a little as incense each day at noon and midnight for seven consecutive days to banish even the most persistent negative forces. Carry a leaf or dried berry in your charm bag, both for protection and to attract the powers of good fortune.

It is obvious that the folk-lore and superstitions surrounding the blackthorn are a result of thousands of years of cultural clashes and we would be well advised to strip away as much of the incoming, or non-native, beliefs as possible when exploring its power. Like most trees, it appears to have both benign and malevolent energies, depending on the period of history to which its folk-lore relates. Whatever we may feel about the tree, it really does herald the beginning of spring in a spectacular fashion.

The leaf, buds and fruit of the blackthorn

Staff or Wand

The blackthorn used as a magical tool has long been associated with cursing. According to Evan John Jones (*Witchcraft—A Tradition Renewed*) "As it is a wood of ill omen, the only use of the black-thorn stang is in the solemn rite of a formal cursing when the coven has to defend itself, or one of its members against an attack from the outside. In this guise, it is the representative of the Two-Faced God. From the same stem comes the power that can be used for both good and evil; a face that should be rarely invoked or worked."

Having said that, there are a number of Old Craft witches whose personal wand is made of blackthorn because this also represents the energies of the goddess in her 'dark of the moon' aspect — in other words the deep, primordial powers of the Wildwood. As with all magic, the power is neutral and the responsibility must therefore rest with the individual and the end for which it is being used. Blackthorn *is* notoriously difficult to control but it should not be viewed as having a sinister or evil reputation.

Mention of a blackthorn rod has featured in several witch trials that when the body of the witch was burned, their blackthorn staff was thrown into the pyre. An ideal offering in payment for a piece of its branch would be a handful of dried fruit.

O X

The box (*buxus sempervirens*) is another native tree that doesn't appear in the tree-alphabet despite the fact that it's been around for a very long time. Box grows naturally on limestone and chalk although there are very few places where actual wild woods of box still exist. Two being Boxwell in Gloucestershire and Box Hill in Surrey where there are a naturally occurring woods. In the distant past, however, the trees must have been much more common, particularly in the south of England where there is the frequency of 'box' or 'bex' in place names confirm its presence.

This is a small tree reaching up to 33 feet in height, but more often growing as a dense, evergreen shrub. In the past its wood was so prized that, according to Geoffrey Grigson's *The English-man's Flora*, the box woods were decimated for their timber. Natural box wood has now become so scarce that in the early 1990s the Society of Wood Engravers mooted the suggestion that box be planted for use of future generations of wood carvers.

Indigenous species, however, are not necessarily native everywhere in the British Isles and the various Forestry Agencies realise that each one is usually of its "highest value to nature conservation when they grow in places where they would occur naturally in the absence of human disturbance or assistance throughout the ages."

According to the conservationists, when creating new woodland, it is best to plant the same native trees that occur in nearby ancient and semi-natural woodland, using only stock of local origin. This means that 'wild' box will only be re-introduced into southern England where "seed collected from semi-natural stands, no further away than, say, 10 miles from where the stock is to be planted" will be used.

Box's yellow, extremely hard and fine-grained wood was the best material for fine wood-engravings of medieval times and for several hundred years until the introduction of steel-engraving. It was also used to make small, decorative boxes, chessmen, musical, mathematical and nautical instruments.

In 995AD, Aelfric, a Benedictine monk of Cerne Abbas, compiled a list of over 200 herbs and trees in which box was listed. It was used for hedging, topiary work and to shelter young plants. A thick screen of box separated the gardens from the main courtyard at Shrewsbury Abbey. The slow-growing, dwarf variety was close clipped (a custom said to have originated with the Romans) to make decorative edgings to formal herb gardens, some of which have been recreated as formal knot gardens.

Although all parts of the tree are poisonous if taken internally (animals have died from eating the leaves) box, taken in small doses, was used as a substitute for quinine in the treatment of recurrent fevers, like malaria. The leaves were used to purify the blood, stimulate hair growth and, together with the bark, to treat rheumatism and dispel intestinal worms. The oil was used to relieve toothache and piles while Pliny recommended the berries for diarrhoea. Both wood and leaves produce an auburn hair dye, while the bark was used in the making of perfume. According to Gerald Wilkinson (*Trees in the Wild*), box wood turner's chips were used by herbalists as the basis of 'hysterical ale', also containing iron filings and a variety of innocuous herbs, it was recommended to be "taken constantly by vapourous women".

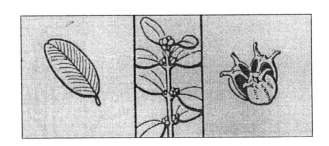

Leaf,
buds
and fruit

ROOT & BRANCH

For some strange reason, in some parts of Britain, box became associated with funerals. In Lancashire box sprigs were handed to the mourners who dropped them into the grave, according to R Vickery, writing for the Folklore Society (*Unlucky Plants*). It was probably due to it being an evergreen and having a rather disagreeable smell when cut, that caused it to be incorporated into the Victorian death-cult rather than any deep-rooted superstition surrounding the tree's history.

From the purely magical point of view there appears to be nothing recorded to give any guidelines as to whether box was included in any magical correspondences or spell working. Since all parts of the tree were known to be poisonous, it would no doubt have been shunned as being unlucky or evil, once its healing propensities had gone out of fashion.

Nevertheless, it is a good idea to have box growing in the garden among the herbs, if only for decorative purposes. Do not be tempted to do a little experimental work with box incense as it can produce the same effects as laurel and, as such must surely represent Elemental Air. This is also born out by the fact that its name *buxus* means flute, and box was used from ancient times for both musical and mathematical instruments.

Staff or Wand

Since box wood is so rare today, it is doubtful whether it would be possible to obtain a full length staff, although a mature shrub might yield up a reasonable sized wand. Because of its rarity, a box wood wand would be a very precious object to both give and receive, although its use would be more ceremonial than magical. An ideal offering would be a libation of fruit juice.

The Tree Alphabet
Beth B Birch
Luis L Rowan
Nion N Ash
Fearn F Alder
Saille S Willow
Uath H Hawthorne
Duir D Oak
Tinne T Holly
Coll C Hazel
Muin M Vine
Gort G Ivy
Pethboc P Dwarf Elder (or Reed)
Ruis R Elder
Ngetal NG Reed
Ailm A Scots Pine or Elm
Onn O Furze/Gorse (or Broom)
Ur U Heather
Eadha E Aspen
Idho I Yew

This is the version that appears in *The White Goddess* to which Robert Graves also added:
Quert Q/CW Apple/Quince
Straif SS/Z Blackthorne
Y Mistletoe

The last being magical to the Celts.
The Apple is the Silver Bough; the Mistletoe, too holy to have a written letter or name, is the Golden Bough, and the Blackthorn is the tree of Magic and the Faere Folk.

herry

There are two indigenous wild cherries in Britain, the bird cherry (*prunus padus*) and the wild cherry (*prunus avium*) although there is an element of confusion between the two. *Prunus avium* – Latin for bird's cherry', is commonly found in most parts of the British Isles as far north as Caithness. Confusingly, *prunus padus*, which is known as the bird's cherry in England, is a northern species, occurring naturally across Scotland, Ireland and northern England.

The wild cherry or gean, is called *idath* in Old Irish, and carries various localised names such as crab cherry, hawkberry, mazzard and merry. This is a tall, handsome tree that can grow to almost 100 feet and when it is covered with snow-white blossom in May it is a magnificent sight, attracting swarms of butterflies and insects. The fruit of the wild cherry, as its name suggests, is black or dark red and although it is not as fleshy or tasty as the cultivated cherry, it is edible. The tree reproduces by sending out suckers to develop into small stands.

The bird cherry is also called black dogwood, black merry and hagberry among many other local names. This is a much smaller tree, rarely reaching a height of 39 feet but when it is in flower, it stands out clearly in ravines and gorges in rugged areas like the Peak District. A solitary tree, the fruit of the bird cherry is too sour to eat with the leaves being poisonous to livestock, particularly goats.

Cherry wood is reddish-brown in colour and can be used for exquisite wood sculpture because of its fine, attractive grain. It is traditionally used for smokers' pipes and is available as joss to perfume the house with a delicate, restful aroma. Choose either cherry wood, which has a more subtle perfume, or cherry which is slightly more fruity.

Strangely enough, there are no historical or oral records of the cherry being associated with folk-lore in Britain although it is listed as the gum being an old remedy for coughs — hence the traditional cherry flavoured cough medicine that is still available. Culpeper wrote that the gum dissolved in wine, "*is good for a cold, cough, and hoarseness of the throat; mendeth the colour in the face, sharpeneth the eye-sight, provoket happetite, and helpeth to break and expel the stone*". The fruit, bark and gum were all used to soothe irritating coughs, treat bronchial complaints and improve digestion. Crushed cherries, applied externally, were reputed to refresh tired skin and relieve migraines.

In the kitchen, the fruit was cooked, eaten raw or pulped with the stones and made into wine, conserves and liqueur. Although the wild cherry listed by Aelfric is a native of Britain, it is believed that the Romans introduced the cultivated variety. Medieval herbalists grafted the more productive varieties on to the rootstock of the wild cherry and in medieval times the fruit was picked when it was wine-red, and eaten ultra-ripe.

Modern medicine has found that certain cherries have proved effective in treating prostate gland enlargement. Looking further a

field, we find that the cherry has long been used by traditional healers from different cultures around the world. With all this information to hand, it is obvious that cherry trees have always been looked upon as providing a domestic service rather than any particular magical use.

Cherry wood (as with all the *prunus* family) gives off a wonderful perfume if the wood is burned on an open fire. If someone is cutting or pruning cherry trees, dry the wood for winter burning or for a Beltaine fire.

Staff or Wand

A cherry wand or staff would be a beautiful gift to give a woman who is a healer and/or priestess because the cherry is obviously a tree with predominantly feminine overtones and so represents Elemental Water. If we have to go searching for correspondences, we find that *"sweet odours are also lunar, because the moon represents the physical senses and refers to the common people. Similarly sugar and sweet things generally are much liked by children (who are classed under Luna)"* If you can find a suitable branch for a wand or staff and perfect libation would be cherry juice or wine.

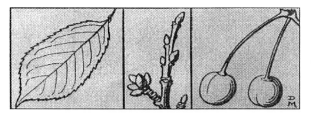

Leaf,
buds and
fruit

The Cherry Tree

Loveliest of trees, the cherry now
Is hung with bloom along the bough,
And stands about the woodland ride
Wearing white for Eastertide.

Now, of my threescore years and ten,
Twenty will not come again,
And take from seventy springs a score,
It only leaves me fifty more.

And since to look at things in bloom
Fifty springs are little room,
About the woodlands I will go
To see the cherry hung with snow.

A E Housman

rab Apple

The crab apple (*malus sylvestris*) must surely be the real 'goddess' tree of the British Isles. It usually occurs singly, scattered throughout almost all types of woodland and hedgerow in eastern England. According to Oliver Rackham in *Trees and Woodland in the British Landscape*, there were roughly one tree for every ten acres in the 1970s. Crab apples can be found throughout Ireland, England and Wales, although they are less common in Scotland.

Crab apple blossom is pinkish-white with an exquisite and delicate perfume. The fruit is small, ranging in colour from yellow to red, with a very sharp taste. Nevertheless, made into crab apple jelly it is an ideal accompaniment to roast pork, or alternatively the fruit can be used to make home-made wine. Old country recipes often say that the addition of a couple of crab apples make all the difference to an apple tart.

Timber from the crab apple can be used for the most delicate of woodcrafts, including engraving and carving. At one time it was the premier wood for making into set-squares and other drawing instruments.

The saying 'an apple a day keeps the doctor away' lays claim to the fruit's health-giving qualities that science now recognises there is

more than a little truth in the saying. In medieval times the fruit was a cure-all; the bark was also used medicinally. The fruit was mainly used to relieve constipation, reduce acidity of the stomach and assist the digestion. Rotten apples were used as a relief for sore eyes.

The cultivated variety of apple were probably introduced into Britain by the Romans and it is believed that the indige-

nous crab apple blossom was white–the pinkish hue being a cor-
ruption of the cultivated variety of apple. During medieval times
the monks increased the number of varieties of 'eating' apple
which became a favourite fruit eaten cooked or raw. They were
also used for making cider, chutneys, sauces, jams and jellies.

Although an indigenous tree, the crab apple appears to have been
in domestic use since ancient times and crab apples were found in
an oaken coffin dating from the early Bronze Age.

The folk-lore associated with it appears mostly to do with deter-
mining romantic outcomes and finding a marriage partner. The
apple has always been regarded as a holy tree and since earliest
times it has been considered very unlucky to destroy apple trees or
an orchard.

On the opposite side of the coin, it was said to bring luck to the
household if several apples were left on the ground after the
harvest to keep the Faere Folk happy. While apple orchards have
long been regarded as places where the realms of the Faere Folk
meet the mundane world.

The Isle of Avalon is often translated to mean 'the island
of apples' and is one of the gateways between the worlds, first mentioned in the 12th century by Geoffrey of Monmouth. Avalon was
the paradise of Welsh legend, presided over by the Queen of the
Faere it was an island of apple trees, situated in the far west where
kings and heroes went after earthly death. It was to Avalon that
Arthur was taken in the Black Ship.

In Celtic mythology, the apple was known as the 'silver bough'.
Mistletoe being the 'golden bough' and, although it is more traditionally associated with oak trees, it is more commonly found on
apple trees. The apple was one of the seven Chieftain trees and
under Brehon law, the unlawful cutting down of an apple tree had
to be paid for with a life.

According to Norse legend, apples are sacred to Idun, the
keeper of the Apples of Immortality and all of the gods had to eat
one of her apples regularly in order to keep their youth and vigour.

Idun is one of the oldest of the Norse deities, very closely linked to Freya, both belonging to the tribe of the Vanir. As guardian of the apples, Idun was also the original guardian of the runes which were carved upon apple wood.

The war-loving Aesir, led by Odin, captured and tortured the holy Vanir priestess, Gullveig to try to get her to reveal her magic, which led to war between the two tribes. For a long time the Aesir were held at bay because of the Vanir's superior magical knowledge but gradually they were overcome and destroyed.

The apple therefore unites the folk-lore and beliefs of most of the pre-christian people of Britain, and as such should be honoured as a holy tree more than it is.

Apples are often referred to in British Witchcraft because when cut across the circumference, the seed cases are set out in the form of a natural pentacle. The five points of the pentacle represent the magical elementals of earth, fire, air, water and spirit and can serve in this capacity on an altar.

Burnt indoors, apple wood will perfume the whole house which certainly makes it one of the woods suitable for the Beltaine fire. Some traditional witches will also use apple juice or cider as a libation in their magical workings and festivities.

Falling apple blossoms can be used for divination in spring. Catch a falling petal and you can use it to make a wish, or catch a dozen and ensure a happy year to come. Make it thirteen if you're counting by lunar months.

Apples also make an appearance at Harvest Home suppers and Samhain when 'bobbing' is a popular entertainment. To use the time to call back spirits of those who have passed from this world during the previous year, choose an unblemished apple and as the clock finishes striking midnight, stick twelve new pins into the apple. Place the apple in the fire and call the name of the person you wish to contact.

The celebrations of Wassail Eve used to be carried out around Winter Solstice but with the introduction of the Gregorian calendar, the date now falls on the 5th January. On this night apple trees were offered libations of cider to encourage fruitfulness in the orchards during the coming year and pieces of bread soaked in cider were placed in the crooks of the trees. Guns were fired to frighten away any evil spirits - but in these post-gun law days, it can be just as effective to use Chinese crackers.

Staff or Wand

As we can see, a wand or staff of apple wood would be ideal for the priestess of a coven because she is symbolically the embodiment of the goddess and also the keeper of hearth and home for the members of her group.   Traditionally apple wands were used in all forms of love magic and represent Elemental Water. When selecting a branch to cut, make sure that you leave a libation of apple juice or cider by way of thanks.

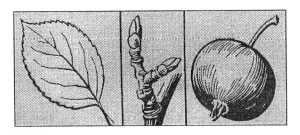

Leaf, buds and fruit

Elder

Although technically classed as a shrub, the elder (*sambucus nigra*) is one of the most useful of our native trees and one of the most widely avoided. For the gardener it is classed as little more than a weed. Both animals and man avoid the ill-smelling leaves. While in folk-lore it is considered to be a most unlucky tree.

For the witch and the countrywoman, however, the elder is known as the 'poor man's medicine chest' having countless uses and representing Elemental Water..

"Elder grows almost anywhere, from heavily polluted roadsides to wind-lashed cliff-tops where it is crusted with salt from the sea spray. It thrives on waste ground, in hedgerows, on heathland, chalk downs, woodland and scrub, and especially where the soil is rich in nitrogen from the manure of animals such as rabbits and badgers. You often see it near drains and sewers – it can be a sign to archaeologists of the site of former dwellings" (*The Patchwork Landscape*).

The dark green leaves which appear in spring keep flies at bay and in the past, they were dried and used as an insecticide, so a sprig of elder hanging up in the house or worn on a hat will send flies packing. Elder leaves make a useful ointment for bruises, sprains and wounds.

The elder in flower is a magnificent sight with its enormous heads of creamy white blossoms with a heady fragrance. While they can be used to make a delicious elderflower champagne, they are used to raise the resistance to respiratory infections. An ointment made from elder flowers is excellent for chilblains and stimulating local circulation. The flowers also make popular hay fever treatments for their anti-catarrhal properties.

The berries are small and green at first, ripening to deep purple clusters that weigh down the branches. These are made into wine, chutney, jellies and ketchup. Medicinally, both the berries and the flowers encourage fever response and stimulates sweating, which prevents very high temperatures and provides an important channel for detoxification.

To cure warts, rub them with a green elder twig which should then be buried. As the wood rots so the wart will disappear.

It is, therefore, quite surprising with all its beneficial properties that the elder gets such a bad press to connect it with all manner of devils, demons and bad 'uns.

Elder has a great number of folk-lore associations. It features in Arthurian tales and has long been associated with witchcraft and religion which might explain why the christians demonised it by having Judas hang himself from its branches and thereby making it a cursed tree! It has been suggested that the name elder derives from the Anglo-Saxon *eldrum*, meaning fire – but this is highly unlikely since elder does not burn very well and most countrymen refused point-blank to burn it on the hearth fire.

In rural areas, the elder has long been referred to as *ellen*-wood which suggests that it was once identified with the Faere Folk. Even country people who would not normally consider themselves superstitious will not cut down an elder tree for fear that bad luck will descend on the house. There have been cases where homeowners have paid an outsider to come and cut the tree down and remove the wood, but this has not prevented bad luck from dogging the house and its inhabitants until the tree grows again.

In many areas of the country there are tales of the Elder Mother or elder spirits who both inhabit the bush and who *are* the tree. Any cavalier treatment of the tree may result in all manner of calamities. It was believed that if a branch was cut and blood spurted from it, then likely as not the village witch was

seen wearing a bandage or walking with a limp. If elder was taken into the house, death would be in the house within a year — put a baby in a cradle made of elder and the Faere Folk would steal it.

These beliefs made it necessary to take very special precautions should anyone wish to gather any wood for magical purposes. The elder should be approached with the head bare in the manner of a supplicant, with folded arms and partially bent legs— in a 'symbolic between the worlds pose with arms and legs neither bent nor straight'.

Let's make no bones about it, with the elder's reputation it is well to remember that you are approaching a very *real* magical and extremely powerful being. Tell the elder why you require its wood and what it will be used for. Wait for permission to be given and be prepared to give some recompense for what you take. A suitable invocation would be:

> *"Lady Ellhorn, give me some of thy wood.*
> *And I will give thee some of mine*
> *When it grows again in the forest."*

Wait for a moment of stillness to occur among the leaves and branches — this being the sign that the tree gives its permission. If there is a violent shaking of the leaves then permission has been denied and you should not proceed. Whatever you cut should then be taken 'wrong handed'.

There are numerous modern tales of the bad luck or illness suffered by those who ignored this warning — and equally good fortune coming the way of those who showed the right amount of reverence. If you have an elder growing in the garden, let it thrive and see how your fortune changes — just have a little word whenever it needs pruning!

The name of the Elder Mother in the above supplication reveals the elder's connection with the Faere Folk and musical instruments as *ellhorn* literally means 'elf horn' i.e. pipes which suggests that the Little People used its wood for that purpose.

Magically the wood is used in personal charms to turn aside curses and banish malevolent spirits from the vicinity. These charms can be placed around the inside of the home for the same purpose. Elder leaves gathered at Beltaine are especially powerful and bunches hung over the doors and windows prevent any negative forces entering. The leaves can also be dried and added to protective pouches although some people find the smell of elder offensive.

The elder has, of course, plenty of otherworld associations. It is the gateway between the worlds — whether the kingdom of the dead or the lands of the Faere Folk — the Elder Mother acts as the gatekeeper. This is why it was believed that sleeping beneath the tree could enable you to make contact with the Mighty Dead; this was also a risky business as it was said that there was the risk of not waking up again!

Rather than run this risk but still be able to utilise the elder's powers when astral journeying, hang a bunch of leaves above the bed and take an infusion of the flowers or berries, - or better still, a glass of elderberry wine.

Staff or Wand

Because of the nature of the tree it is perhaps unwise to use it as a wand or staff; also because it is not very strong when dried.

Elder leaves, buds and fruit

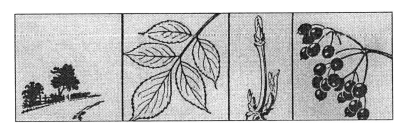

ROOT & BRANCH

awthorn

There are two indigenous types of hawthorn, the common, (*crataegus monogyna*) and Midland hawthorn (*crataegus laevigata*). The former is found throughout the country, except in the far north of Scotland. It thrives on most soils, in open habitats such as hillsides, neglected pasture, on commons, in woodlands and most hedgerows. The Midland hawthorn is mostly confined to the east Midlands and south-east England where it is often found in the shrub layer of oak woods.

The leaves of the common hawthorn have distinct lobes and indentations that may reach as far as the midrib, with the tips of the lobes serrated. The leaves of the Midland hawthorn are more rounded, with small lobes and shallow indentations. The leaves of both trees have a nutty flavour and used to be eaten by children as 'bread and cheese'.

The hawthorn blossoms in May (hence its familiar name), when the trees are smothered in clusters of white blossoms that give out a strangely disturbing but unmistakable perfume. The berries, known as haws, turn red in late August and last well into the winter to produce vital food for the birds, who in turn scatter the seeds away from the parent tree.

Common hawthorn has been used for about 2000 years as natural barbed fencing because its tangle of thorny branches makes an ideal barrier for enclosing and protecting livestock. Its name derives from the Anglo-Saxon *haegthorn*, which means hedge-tree and signs of defensive hawthorn hedges have been discovered round the edges of excavated Roman forts.

The natural life-span for a hawthorn is around 100 years but some have reached the ripe old age of 300 years. Slow growth produces a very hard wood and although it burns well, hawthorn timber is little used today except for tool handles and walking sticks.

Medicinally, the hawthorn can rival the elder. Culpeper recommends pounded or bruised and boiled seeds as cures for various internal pains, probably because they and the dried flowers can reduce blood pressure and circulatory problems. A compote of fresh fruits was given as a cure for diarrhoea. *"The seeds in the berries beaten to powder being drunk in wine, are good against the stone and dropsy. The distilled water of the flowers stays the lax. The seeds cleared of the down and bruised, being boiled in wine, are good for inward pains."*

In modern herbalism the properties of some of the hawthorn's active constituents are now better understood and present a remarkable picture of what is known as synergy — meaning 'working together'. Some constituents strengthen the heart's action, others slow it slightly and improve the blood supply. The net effect is to make a weak heart work more effectively and to reduce blood pressure. An infusion of 5gm of dried flowers and leaves per cup must be taken three times a day, long-term, to have any significant effect.

For culinary use, hawthorn berries or flowers were used to make jellies, wines, liqueurs and sauces.

Hawthorn has perhaps more connections with ancient beliefs, folklore and traditions than almost any other native tree in the British Isles apart from the blackthorn The appearance of the blossom at the beginning of May in the Gregorian calendar (May Day was on what is now 12th May in the old Julian calendar) heralded the end of winter and the beginning of summer. It was said to be unlucky to take may flowers into the house because the Faere Folk are believed to live inside or under the trees — especially those growing on grassy mounds.

For the Romans, however, the hawthorn was a symbol of hope and protection, and cuttings were brought into the home to ward

off evil spirits. It also echoed the ancient British tradition that the tree was associated with marriage and fertility. Pliny wrote that "there are some who maintain that women who take the flower in drink conceive within 40 days".

An old country rhyme recommends the tree as protection for man and animals in thunderstorms:

> *Beware the oak—it courts the stroke.*
> *Beware the ash—it courts the flash.*
> *Creep under the thorn—it will save you from harm.*

Like the elder, the hawthorn was also looked upon as a doorway to otherworld and perhaps it is this association and its links with the old pagan festivals that give the tree its 'unlucky' reputation. As is often found, there is more than a grain of truth in old wives tales. Quite recently it was discovered that one of the chemicals that make up the flowers' sweet scent is also produced during the decay of corpses. On the other hand, the fragrance of the blossom is also reputed to have a strong aphrodisiac effect, particularly on men.

Taking all things into account, it would appear that the pre-christian view of the hawthorn was one of protection. It is appropriate to use hawthorn for the Beltaine bonfires, which the cattle were driven through and the villagers leapt over to ensure their fertility in the coming year. Make a wish as you leap a hawthorn fire, but keep it secret to ensure that it will come true.

The tree can also be used to protect babies and young children. Hang a sprig above a child's bed to bring them under the protection of the goddess/guardian, or keep a pouch of the leaves sewn into the pillow.

Hawthorn can also be planted by the home to keep out evil or negative influences and protect it from lightning strikes. It was also said that cattle thrived in fields where hawthorn grew. Make a wash of flowers and leaves to sprinkle around the house to repel evil spirits and negative energies. The wood, berries and leaves can also be burnt in incense form to purify and attract beneficent energies.   An infusion of berries (known as haws or hags) gives added protection when dispelling negative energies.   In times of trouble or depression take an infusion of the flowers or leaves, or burn them as incense.

To make a Hawthorn Ball
On New Year's Day the women of the house should cut a selection of long, thin branches of hawthorn and plait them into a sphere. This should be dried in the oven/hearth and suspended in the kitchen until the following New Year.   While the women of the household were making a new ball, the men would take the old hawthorn ball out into the fields and set light to it.   According to tradition, it should be carried so that pieces of the burning haw-thorn fall into the furrows in order to bring life and fertility to the crops.   For a special charm to bring good fortune into your home, burn the ball in the garden and when it has been rendered down to ash, sprinkle the remains around the boundary of your property for good luck.

Staff or Wand
Hawthorn is said to be sacred to the powers of Elemental Fire and any demon or malevolent spirits can be controlled with a wand of hawthorn.   This is one of the trees of the *White Goddess*, Cardia who casts her enchantments with a hawthorn wand.   Make sure to leave a suitable offering if you take any wood from the tree — perhaps bread or cheese.

Leaf, bud and berries

Hazel

The hazel (*corylus avellana*) has always been a major coppice tree and was listed by Aelfric in his *Nominum Herbarum.* It was one of the first trees to grow widely in Britain soon after the last glacial period. In the fossilised pollen records preserved in peat which are our guide to the earliest native plants after the Ice Age, hazel predominates over much of the British Isles — appearing at much the same time as the initial spread of other wind-pollinated trees such as willow, alder and birch. In fact, studies have shown that there was seventeen times the amount of hazel pollen in the air at one point, than the total pollen from all other trees in Britain.

The hazel belongs to the same family as the hornbeam, which has more scaly catkins and winged nutlets. The hazel leaf is a dense, green colour which turns to brown and then yellow-gold in the autumn. The brownish-yellow catkins (lamb's tails) begin to develop in the autumn and burst into flower in the spring, dangling from the leafless twigs and releasing clouds of golden pollen.

At least two hazel trees growing close together are needed for fertilisation and the production of nuts. This is because the female catkin usually ripens after the male flower of the same tree. The hazel can be seen as a harbinger of spring, displaying its cascades of golden flowers against the sombre backdrop of the wood. Beware of bringing sprays of catkins indoors as the falling pollen can mark furniture.

Hazel cobs were eaten raw, and used in cakes, bread and confectionery and liqueurs in the Middle Ages., while oil from the nuts was used in cooking. The indigenous cobnut (or filbert), however has become almost an endangered species although some 250 acres of the original 7,000 acres in Kent still produce an annual crop. The Romans used them to flavour roast duck and the Victorians considered them an important ingredient for soups, roasts and puddings, often serving them as an after-dinner accompaniment to port.

Cobnuts are only sold fresh and although some folk prefer to pick them while the shells are still green at the beginning of the season (late August) the majority will leave them until the shells turn brown (mid October). They are larger versions of the hazel nut although the kernel has a sweeter taste, more like sweet chestnuts. The nuts are high in vitamin E and calcium and can be used in autumn recipes such as baked marrow stuffed with tomatoes.

A recipe using these as ingredient would be an ideal accompaniment to the Sunday roast or as part of your magical workings to find a close friend or lover. Share a double nut with them although you must both eat the nuts in silence for the charm to work properly. There are lots of magical associations with the hazel tree which has been linked with wisdom, magic and divination for centuries.

Remains of hazel nut shells have been found at the bottom of peat deposits, suggesting that the early Stone Age hunters were probably at least partly dependent on the hazel nuts for food, in the absence of any sort of cereal. Since prehistoric times the long flexible twigs of 'withies' of the trees have been used to bind bundles, weave baskets, make hurdles and build coracles. In medieval times the twigs were used for the 'wattle' or panels, in wattle and daub buildings. The brushwood was bundled into faggots that were used for the weekly firing of bread ovens.

The hazel was considered sacred in Celtic mythology as one of the Chieftain Trees, and symbolised fertility and immortality. Since hazel is associated with man's earliest ancestors, it is perhaps not surprising that in Celtic folk-lore it was also known as the Tree of Knowledge and, as such was supposed to have many magical properties. There are several important Celtic myths surrounding the association of knowledge and wisdom and, like the apple, it was a capital offence to destroy a hazel tree. It was "the only breathing thing paid for only with breathing things" - meaning that a life

would be demanded to recompense for the fallen tree. Irish aches and pains caused by the damp climate – or elfin malevolence – were thought to be warded off by a hazel nut carried in the pocket.

The bark, leaves, and fruit of the hazel had various medicinal uses, including the treatment of varicose veins, circulatory disorders, menstrual problems, rheumatism, haemorrhoids and slow-healing wounds. Culpeper wrote that the nuts, sprinkled with pepper 'draws rheum from the head'. Hazel oil was used for soap and cosmetics. Hazel nuts are a wonderful gift for a new bride – as long as she wants plenty of children!

An incense made from the fruit or twigs can be used for almost all magical purposes, particularly to strengthen mental powers. It is especially effective for aiding magical Will and concentration, also to give the stamina needed to complete long or complicated rituals. Hazel is associated with Elemental Air and was one of the nine sacred woods used to kindle the Need-Fire at Beltaine.

Weave a wreath of leaves and twigs to place in your sacred space during magical working to gain your most secret wishes and desires. Most of the spells given in folk-lore and modern grimoires concentrate on love charms but these can be adapted to suit most requests, including banishment.

Hazel nuts can be used in love philters, when they will awaken the recipient to the virtues of the sender. On the other hand, if you want a person out of your life, simply chant repeatedly "Depart! Depart! Depart!" as you fix their image in your mind's eye and cast hazel leaves into the fire.

The nuts can also be used for divinational purposes especially for asking questions relating to partnerships (business, personal, etc,). Place two hazel nuts side by side on the bars of the fire grate. If they burn together, all is well. If one nut burns, the partnership is one-sided. If they both fail to burn it could be time for you to be looking to discontinue the partnership. If one or both nuts explode, give it up as a bad job anyway!

Hazel catkins

Hazel nuts can be used to gain the aid of Nature spirits or to make contact with the Faere Folk.   Make a necklace of nuts and either wear it when you go into the countryside, or hang it in your home or sacred area to attract the deities of the Greenwood.

Staff or Wand

Although we think of the forked hazel twig as the diviner's rod, these days a straight hazel wand can also be used for water divining and to attract rain, despite the fact that it represents Elemental Air. To protect a seed bed from the birds, insects and the Faere Folk, draw an equal-armed cross followed by a heart and another cross, with a hazel wand.

Because of its magical powers associated with wisdom and divination, the wood was used to make a sorcerer's wands. The most potent hazel wand should be cut on a Midsummer's morning and the carrying of a hazel wand conferred not only wisdom but the power of eloquence on the bearer.   Leave an offering of sweet bread flavoured with nuts.

ᕼolly

The holly (*ilex aquifolium*) is probably the most recognisable of all our native trees and is found mostly in parks and gardens and woodland. Holly is also the important evergreen in the traditional pagan custom of Yule indoor decoration, symbolising the continuation of life during winter dormancy. The old carole reminds us that:

> *The holly and the ivy, when they are both full grown,*
> *Of all the tress in the Greenwood, the holly wears the crown.*

This is because the holly is sacred to the Horned God in his guise as the Holly King, Lord of the waning year, who takes precedence until the Winter Solstice. It is also sacred to Mother Hel, the Norse goddess of the underworld. It represents Elemental Fire.

The holly is dioecious, bearing sparse winter flowers in early summer that are pollinated by bees. These flowers first appear when the tree is around 20 years old but the splendid display of scarlet berries on the female trees do not occur until the tree has reached 40 years.

Despite being poisonous to humans, the berries sustain the local bird population through the winter when other food is hard to come by. For a variety of reasons, the berries stay on the tree longer than on others and do not spoil or fall off, even after a severe frost. Very often you will find that individual holly trees are vigorously defended by a pair of thrushes who seem to treat the tree as their own private larder.

In the Middle Ages, holly proved to be a useful tree for both peasants and farmers since, in spite of the prickly leaves, the upper foliage of mature trees provided nutritious fodder for domestic animals and deer. Historically, it was coppiced and pollarded for this purpose and is still carried out today to feed sheep and cows during harsh weather conditions.

Holly is often found in old hedges dating back to before 1700 and across the country there are relics of medieval holly woods which were widespread in England, Ireland and Scotland. According to Oliver Rackham in *Ancient Woodland*, holly woods appear to have been peculiar to Britain and so for the witch these rare sites offer an ideal sacred space in which to work.

The timber from the tree is white and fine grained, although it is very heavy — even sinking in water. It stains and polishes well, often being used for chessmen, the hammers in harpsichords, the butts for billiard cues and fine engraving. It was apparently used by the Celts to make chariot shafts and, according to Brehon Law, that was why the holly was one of the Chieftain Trees.

When boiled and fermented, the bark makes a sticky substance known as 'birdlime', which was used to trap small birds. This method is often referred to in period novels and history books.

The berries of the holly are highly toxic and can cause serious bouts of vomiting and diarrhoea. This can be particularly dangerous for children who may find the bright, shiny berries irresistible. In professional use, the leaves are infused to help to treat colds and coughs and have diuretic properties that relieve urinary infections. They are also used as a fever remedy and have some therapeutic action in the treatment of jaundice and rheumatism. Despite its many applications, holly should only be used medicinally under strict professional supervision and should never be used as a self-help treatment or for children. Despite these warnings, many modern herbals encourage the use of holly berries as a purgative. You have been warned!

Needless to say, it is unlucky to cut down a holly tree, especially in Ireland where it is also held to be sacred to the Faere Folk. Because of this connection, it is said to be inadvisable to grow holly near the house. In England, however, it used to be planted close to the home to ward off lightning, as well as to repel witches and poison — which according to beliefs of the time, meant the same thing!

Aside from good luck that the tree brings when growing near the house, the holly is a weather omen; when the branches are heavily laden with berries, it is a sign of a hard, snowy winter to come.

Holly has been used as a Yule decoration for centuries and was used for the same purpose at the Roman Saturnalia. Exiled Romans would still have celebrated the festivals of their homeland even if the British climate was a little cold for Roman revels. Because of the tree's pagan associations, the early church attempted to ban its use, but without success.

The wood of the holly gives off a hot fire but burns very quickly. It can, however, be burnt 'green' (i.e. freshly cut), without waiting for it to dry out.

The kind of holly brought into a couple's home for their first Yule together will dictate who will wear the trousers. He-holly, with the sharp prickles, means the man will be the boss; she-holly (without prickles or only very soft ones) means that the woman will rule the roost. Some superstitions say this is the way it will be, while others say it only lasts until the next Yule when fresh holly is brought home.

Magically, holly is used primarily to keep intruders at bay, deflect negative energies and rebound spells to the sender. On the first count it makes an effective boundary hedge as very few people would be willing to push their way through a holly hedge. Use holly in charm bags and incense for all defensive rituals and, in times of greatest danger, position sprigs of holly around the boundary of your home to keep out negative forces. Holly also works well as a protection for domestic animals. Fasten some to an animal's collar to keep it safe when away from your protective influences, and be sure to hang a sprig in any barns or stables where animals are kept. This helps them thrive and wards off the attentions of the Faere Folk. One country superstition says that if you throw a sprig of holly after a run-away animal, it will return of its own accord.

Staff or Wand

Holly wood makes an excellent staff or wand because it is an undiluted symbol of male energies. When out walking at night, a holly staff will keep you safe from all mischievous entities and at one time, no coachman would drive after sunset unless the handle of their whip was fashioned from holly wood. A wand made out of holly is also helpful in keeping unruly spirits under control. An offering of spiced wine might be appropriate if the staff or wand is cut at Winter Solstice.

Male leaf, buds and berries

ornbeam

The hornbeam (*carpinus betulus*) grows as a native tree in the oak woodlands of southern England and is noted for its compact stature and its magnificent yellow and red-gold autumn colours. As the climate became warmer after the last Ice Age, Britain was colonised by trees which spread across from the Continent. The pollen records show that the hornbeam was a relative latecomer, arriving about 5000 years ago, whereas the oak was already widespread 2500 years earlier.

Unfortunately, the hornbeam is not at all well known, and unless a search is made for it and an idea gained of what it may look like, it may quite easily be passed by as it can be mistaken for a beech tree. In fact, it also goes by the names of horse beech, hurst beech and white beech and, as such can be associated with Elemental Earth.

Left to their own devices, hornbeam will spread their branches as widely as beech and, when allowed to grow unhindered, mature into a really impressive tree of between 30 to 70 feet. One way of telling the difference between the two trees is that the bark of the hornbeam is furrowed, as if with swollen veins, whereas the beech is smooth. The flowers come about the same time as the leaves in

April and May and, unless carefully looked for, will not be seen. These are yellowish male catkins, very similar to those of the hazel, while the female catkins are much longer and looser. The fruit grows in bunches and are small, brown nuts enclosed in a leafy, three-lobed 'scale'. The seeds ripen in October or November. Like the beech, the leaves often remain on the tree throughout the winter.

The hornbeam has the hardest wood of any tree in Europe. It is yellowish-white wood, tough and hard, yet it is light and flexible. Craftsmen have made little use of it for furniture or cabinet-making because it is too hard — their tools were blunted so quickly that much time was wasted in re-sharpening them. Nevertheless it has been used for heavy-duty purposes in making agricultural tools, cogs, portions of pianos, cogs and pulleys.

Although the wood is extremely tough it burns well and before coal became the major source of energy, hornbeams were regularly coppiced and pollarded to provide wood and charcoal for fuel. It also had a specific use for bakers because on Saturday the oven would be fuelled with this wood and, due to its slow burning, the oven would be hot enough for baking on Monday morning. This avoided criticism from the Church about working on a Sunday, whilst allowing the baker to go about his normal weekday business.

Staff or Wand

Although there appears to be no references to the hornbeam in folk-lore, the tree does have a certain rarity value and can probably be credited with the same attributes as the beech. It's greatest symbol would be strength. A bread or biscuit flavoured with nuts would be appropriate as an offering.

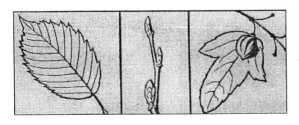

Leaf, buds and fruit

Pollarding

When visiting a wood you should look for signs, particularly in the shapes of the trees, that tell of the history of the wood and what it has been used for.

Pollarding refers to trees that have been cut to produce successive crops of wood at a height of 6-15 feet above the ground so that grazing animals cannot reach the young shoots. Pollarding is carried out on wood-pasture and hedgerows rather than those in woods.

From the historical perspective, pollarding allowed livestock to graze the common land of the parish, which often included woodland. As a result, this type of wood-pasture developed its own appearance. It has a bare grassy floor (for the animals destroyed the spring flowers and undergrowth) and the trees were well spaced out because the animals also ate many of the new saplings. Supplies of poles could still be obtained by cropping the branches of the trees at head height and this became known as 'pollarding' from the word mean 'head'.

Old pollarded trees can still be seen today and although the technique has all but died out, it has been well documented since Anglo-Saxon times. Apart from wood-pasture, many old pollards can be found in hedges, in farmland as boundary markers, or along water-courses (pollard willows or poplars).

Coppicing

The word coppice comes from the French, *couper*, meaning to cut. When shrubs and young trees are cut back to the ground they quickly sprout a head of shoots which grow about 6 feet high in a year and then begin to thicken. The resulting plant is called a coppice.

After about seven to fifteen years the shoots of the coppice used to be cut to provide a supply of poles, staves and brushwood. Scattered throughout the coppices were the standard trees which had been allowed to grow unhindered until they reached an ago of about 70-150 years when they were felled for timber.

The most obvious signs of past coppicing is the presence of 'many-trunked' trees growing on the site of old coppice stumps. It was also important in past times to keep livestock out since they would destroy the young shoots and so the wood was often surrounded by a ditch with a large bank inside, which was often fenced. The remains of the bank and ditch can still be seen in places.

Another clue to woods that were once coppiced is the abundance of spring flowers. The regular cutting of the coppices allowed plenty of light to reach the woodland floor and this encouraged the growth of the plants. Woodland flowers are slow to spread and so their presence in large numbers is an excellent indication that the wood is ancient and was once coppiced.

Juniper

Juniper (*juniperus communis*) - our only native member of the Cypress family — has the greatest world range of any conifer. It arrived soon after the last glacial period and spread throughout the British Isles as far north as the Orkneys. Except for the Chiltern escarpment where there is quite a lot of juniper scrub, today it grows mainly in Scotland and southern England, usually as a low-growing shrub, except for a few scattered locations in Ireland, north Wales and northern England.

Its habitat, however, is mixed. In southern England, where it is in decline, it grows on the chalk-down grasslands, especially on steeper hillsides where the soil is shallow. In Scotland it is found in native Scots pine forests, birchwoods and on heather moorland. On high mountains it sometimes forms low-growing scrub just above the tree line. Of the juniper poet, Laurance Binyon wrote:

> *"The slope is darkly sprinkled*
> *With ancient junipers,*
> *Each a small secret tree:*
> *There not a branch stirs."*

The juniper grows slowly, its branches densely packed with narrow

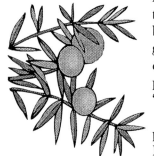

needle-like leaves arranged in whorls of three. In some ways the juniper resembles the yew and they frequently grow together on the steep-sided ridges and combes on southern downland. In some parts of Wales it is referred to as the 'dwarf yew'.

The juniper 'flowers' in May or June, producing both male and female cones. In autumn the female cones swell to form a hard green berry which remain on the bush for two or three years, gradually ripening into fleshy, blue-black berries, coated with a greyish bloom like the sloe.

Despite its small state, the timber from the juniper is extremely tough and was in demand for decorative veneers. After a good polish, the wood gleams a rich red colour. In the Lake District the wood made the charcoal that was used for gunpowder.

Famed for its medicinal uses, Pliny wrote that the juniper, "even above all other remedies, is warming and alleviates symptoms". Roman physicians prescribed it for pains in the stomach, chest and side, flatulence, coughs and colds, tumours and disorders of the uterus. Some even suggested smearing the body with an extract from the seeds as a protection against snake bites.

Culpeper recommended the berries for a great variety of ailments, ranging from an antidote against poisons and a defence against the plague, to strengthening the brain and curing 'wind from any part of the body'. Its country name of bastard killer arose from eating of the berries to procure an abortion. Juniper berries should not be taken during pregnancy, or by those with kidney problems.

In modern herbalism juniper is used internally to treat cystitis, urethritis, kidney inflammation, rheumatism, gout, arthritis and poor digestion with wind and colic. Externally it is used for rheumatic pain and neuralgia. There is an additional warning that it may cause skin irritation and allergic responses.

For culinary purposes, in medieval times, oil of juniper, made from the sharp-tasting berries, was used to flavour liqueurs (notably gin), and added to marinades, stews, sauces, and certain meat dishes. The berries can be added to pickles, game, patés, ham and pork. The wood was burned to smoke preserved meats. The berries also yield a brown dye.

In classical times, the branches were burned as a purifying herb in temples; in Britain branches were strewn on the floors to sweeten the smell of rooms, and burned to cleanse the air of disease and

infection, especially during epidemics. An incense made from juniper leaves and berries would obviously be ideal for cleansing or banishing rituals. [In more recent times, juniper was favoured by those involved in the illicit distilling of spirits because the dry wood burns with very little smoke.]

Sprigs of juniper should be hung over the doorways at Beltaine and Samhain to keep out any negative energies or troublesome spirits. The incense can also be used for divinational purposes for seeing into the future.

Staff or Wand

In many parts of the country juniper was considered a powerful protection against 'witches, devils and evil spirits', so a wand made from its wood would make an ideal 'blasting rod' for banishments. The wood was also used for the handles of daggers and could be used as a handle for the witch's knife—as such it should be associated with Elemental Fire. An ideal offering when taking the wood would be a slice of raw meat or a libation of gin!

Guessing the age of the woods

Many of the woods that were once pollarded or coppiced are extremely ancient.. Trackways across the marshy areas of Somerset were built of poles which have been identified as coppiced alder, ash, holly and hazel dating from 2500BC.

Trees of many different kinds, with oak probably dominant, indicates an old woodland. All the trees are native though sycamore may have been introduced at a much later date. Trees of one kind (such as oak or beech) growing close together with tall trunks, perhaps planted in rows, indicates high forest plantation more than 100 years old.

If the woodland is old it was once either coppiced or grazed. If the woods were grazed (I.e. used as wood-pasture) the trees would have been pollarded, so look for old pollards and a lack of variety in ground plants as the clues to old wood-pasture.

Look to see if there is nothing but grass under the trees. This suggests that grazing continues. Wood-pasture is a dead tradition but some old northern coppice woods are now used for sheltering and grazing sheep.

Look for signs of previous coppicing: perhaps there are 'many-trunked' trees growing from the site of the old coppice stools. The main point is that a wood that was being coppiced 100 years ago is likely to be an old wood. The small-leaved lime is another good Indicator, while the Midland hawthorn shows that the old coppiced area has never been anything but woodland.

Lime

Small-leafed lime (*tilia cordata*) or linden trees are tolerant of most soil conditions and can withstand hard pruning, which is why they are most commonly found in the streets of our towns and inner cities.

According to research carried out by Cambridge University, however, although natural lime trees may not be a very familiar sight for most of us, the ancient limes in the north-west of England have a very interesting history and are probably well over 1000 years old. From the pollen records it is abundantly clear that the lime was the dominant tree species in the forests of England, they reached their maximum extent around 5,500 years ago.

The pollen records also show that the area in which high frequencies of lime occurred, when the forest cover was at its greatest, coincides with the natural location of the tree today. The Lake District, where ancient limes can be found, is now known to be the northern-most limit of the tree's original distribution.

Lime trees began their decline shortly after the major decline in elm, which began about 5,100 years ago, and is thought to have been associated with forest clearance and introduced woodland grazing. Today, many ancient limes are found in particularly inaccessible locations, which is probably why they have survived the various forest clearances of the past.

Evidence of limes being in a location in the past can be traced by place names. For example Linsty Wood, where the limes were a 'conspicuous feature in the 10th century, as the name contains the Norse elements 'lind' and 'stigr', meaning a path where the lime-trees grow (*The Tree Book*). The small-leafed lime trees found in natural woodland also mean that the woods themselves are old.

Lime trees can look just as impressive in winter with their bare branches as they can in summer, cloaked in leaves. As Percival Westell wrote in his book on *Trees*:

"True we all love the honeyed scent of the limes on a warm summer day, and so do the countless legions of bees who croon among its wealth of flowers for hours at a stretch. We also admire its early autumn coat of yellow. But is it not as well to look at the lime when one can see its pliant branches in winter bearing their tight reddish buds, each one, when rain falls or hoar frost melts as the sun shines, being like a diamond at anchor?"

The timber is prized for its pale colour and its suitability for carving, turning and musical instruments.

In modern herbalism, the flowers of the lime are used as a sedative, a relaxant,, an antispasmodic and a vasodilator (an agent that widens and relaxes blood vessels) and with their mild, pleasant taste, lime flowers are among the most popular herbal relaxants. The flowers produce an aromatic mucilaginous herb that is diuretic and expectorant; it calms the nerves, lowers blood pressure, increases the perspiration rate, relaxes spasms and improves the digestion. Taken as an infusion for hypertension, hardening of the arteries, cardiovascular and digestive complaints associated with

The lime in summer

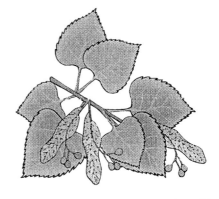

anxiety, urinary infections, feverish colds, influenza, respiratory catarrh, migraine and headaches.

To harvest lime flowers, pick while they are still young in the summer and dry them for use in infusions, liquid extracts and tinctures. For an infusion: use 2 teaspoons per cup, infused for no more than five minutes.

Warning: Lime flowers develop narcotic properties as they age and should only be collected when first opened. Infusions made from old, stale leaves can sometimes cause sensations of drunkenness.

Despite the lime's impressive history as an indigenous tree and its multi-layered medicinal uses, it is surprising that the lime does not play any significant part in British folk-lore apart from the belief that lime flowers cured epilepsy if the sufferer sat under the tree. Perhaps with its associations with healing it should represent Elemental Air.

Staff or Wand:
Cut the staff or wand as a gift for a healer as the tree's beneficial properties are of paramount importance. Pour a libation of a linden flower infusion sweetened with honey.

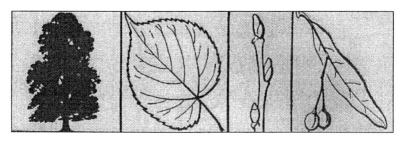

Old Country Rhyme

Beechwood fires are bright and clear.
If logs are kept a year;
Chestnut only good they say,
If for long it's laid away;
Make a fire of elder tree,
Death within your house shall be;
But ash new or ash old
Is fit for Queen with crown of gold.

Birch and fir logs burn too fast,
Blaze up bright and do not last;
It is by the Irish said
Hawthorn bakes the sweetest bread'
Elmwood burns like churchyard mould ~
E'en the very flames are cold;
But ash green or ash brown
Is fit for Queen with golden crown.

Poplar gives a bitter smoke,
Fills your eyes and makes you choke;
Apple wood will scent your room
With an incense-like perfume;
Oaken logs, if dry and old,
Keep away the winter's cold;
But ash wet or ash dry
A King shall warm his slippers by.

Maple

Field maple (*acer campestre*) can be found in woodlands and hedgerows throughout England, often growing as an 'under-storey tree'. Its distinctive paired leaves are five-lobed, downy when young and a dark green when mature. Unlike the other species of maple, the foliage does not turn scarlet in autumn, but remain an attractive bright yellow-ish green, retaining its leaves for several weeks up to December. It is widespread in southern and eastern England, but less common in western and northern counties. Although it is generally a small tree, it can grow to a height of thirty feet if left to its own devices.

The leaves are much smaller than the more easily recognisable foreign species and can often be mistaken for the sycamore. The trunk is covered with pale greyish-brown bark which in older trees is furrowed with a series of cracks; even the twigs develop ridges of gnarled bark. The field maple flowers in May or June, shortly after the leaves have unfolded, producing clusters of small greenish-yellow blossoms.

Maple wood was highly prized by wood-turners and cabinet-makers who specialised in fine articles, as it could be cut so fine as

to be almost transparent. The pale brown timber with its well marked grain is still valued by craftsmen. In ancient times it was used for making harps like those found in ancient Saxon barrows, including the Sutton Hoo burial.

Like many members of the acer family, the field maple produces a sweet sap in the spring that can be used for making wine or maple syrup. The brilliant autumn colours displayed by maples result from the unusually high concentration of sugar in the leaves and sap. Sugar can be extracted from the wood by boiling and Culpeper recommended decoctions of the leaves or the bark for 'strengthening the liver'.

There is very little recorded about the maple in British folk-lore and yet again, the tree has been around for a very long time. Pollen records show that around 5,000 years ago, the areas of heavy, or calcareous soil, were in all probability, dominated by ash, hazel, maple and elm.

Was the maple a sacred tree in England in pre-Celtic times and, like the alder and aspen conveniently over-looked when it came to constructing the Tree Alphabet on which much of today's tree-lore is based? Records trace it back to the Neolithic period and its use as a fodder tree; *mapuldur* was its Old English name. Maple-wood tables were valuable collector's items in the Roman world, one being sold for its weight in gold.

Maple leaves

ROOT & BRANCH

Like the alder and aspen, using the maple for magical working is a matter for experimentation but as it is said to bring 'expansive, happy energy' to any situation, it may possibly be associated with Elemental Air. If we gather the glorious 'guinea-gold' coloured leaves for the autumn equinox, perhaps the tree could begin to play a part in a traditional Harvest Home.

Staff or Wand

The wood from the roots of the field maple, with its beautiful swirling pattern of veins, shows up well when polished and it is unlikely that you will be able to cut more than a small wand from the tree. In other cultures the maple symbolises positive thinking and the use of intuition and so a wand made from it could be used to direct meditation. An ideal offering would be a sweet syrup.

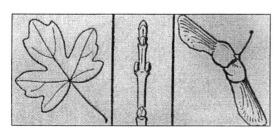

*Field maple leaf,
buds and seeds*

Trees in the Hedgerows

It's not just the woods that can be dated from the variety and number of different species, British hedgerows have their own history and this is also chronicled by certain tell-tale signs.

Hedgerows were probably originally planted to mark ancient boundaries, to estates and parishes, for example.. The majority, however, were planted in the 18th and 19th centuries to enclose patches of land in order to establish ownership or control live-stock.

Hawthorn is the most common tree to be found in the hedgerow, although many included black-thorn and holly. Other species arrive as seeds—dog rose and ash soon appear while others, like hazel and field maple are very slow to colonise.

A hedge planted as pure hawthorn slowly acquires additional species as it gets older and scientific studies of the species diversity of hedge-rows in relation to their age (where this can be reasonably accurately dated from historical records), have shown that there is more or less a direct relationship between the number of species established in a hedge and its age.

As a general rule one new species colonises the hedge every 100 years, so that a two-species hedge could be 200 years old and a ten-species hedge 1000 years old.

Oak

There are two native oaks in Britain, the pedunculate (*quercus robur*) and the sessile (*quercus petraca*) oaks trees make up one tenth of all English woods.
The trees can be told apart by the over-all shape of the tree and by the leaves.

When growing in the open, the pedunculate oak is gnarled and tends to have lower, more horizontal and wide-spreading branches, so that the main trunk is hidden beneath a mass of boughs and leaves. The leaves themselves are pale green with two obvious 'ear-lobes' at the base, with deep indentations all round. The sessile oak has a straighter, less gnarled trunk, with branches growing from higher up. Its leaves are dark green, have no 'ear-lobes' and the indentations are not so deep.

The oak may not come into leaf until mid-May and there may even be a second bursting of leaves known traditionally as the 'Lammas budding' since it tends to coincide with the Lammas festival on 1st August.

Of all British trees, the oak supports the widest variety of insect and other vertebrate life and more fungi are associated with the oak than with any other native tree. "Like a crowded high rise block, the oak is inhabited at every level: birds and squirrels build nests in the crown, insects such as wasps, moths, beetles and weevils devour the leaves; ivy, mistletoe, lichens, mosses, algae and fungi invade the branches and bark; birds, insects and mammals feed on the acorns. Even the roots of the young oak are sought out by such insects as weevils and, as the oak lets in quite a lot of light through its leaves, flowering plants grow underneath it." (*The Ever-changing Woodlands*)

From the historical perspective, oak woods covered much of Britain in medieval times and our ancestors quickly discovered that oak made good fuel. From the Middle Ages until the 18th century people drove their pigs into the oak woods on common land to feed on the fallen acorns. Such grazing rights still exist in the New Forest. Oak was used extensively for ship building and for supporting beams in country cottages.

The oak has featured in most of the major folk-beliefs. Sir James Frazer, in *The Golden Bough*, maintained that "The worship of the oak tree or of the oak god appears to have been shared by all the branches of the Aryan stock in Europe."

The oak appears to have a great affinity (or attraction) for lightning and is sacred to all storm-gods, such as Jupiter and Thor. The Dagda carried a club made from an oak tree, and the Horned God, especially in his guise as Jack-in-the-Green with his foliate mask (as the god of green and growing things), made up of oak leaves and acorns. In Welsh the tree is called *pren awyr* which means 'celestial tree' or 'tree of heaven'.

The close grain of the timber means that the wood burns slowly and give s out a lot of heat. But it was its association with gods of lightning that gave it its associations with Elemental Fire. Oak was also the sacred wood burnt by the Druids for the midsummer sacrifice, kindled by rubbing together two oak sticks. The fires of Vesta, Roman goddess of hearth and home, were kept eternally burning, fed by oak. Magical need-fires were started with a brand of burning oak; and the Yule log lit at the Winter solstice (a piece of which should be kept to light the next year's fire) was oak.

Sessile oak leaf

Medicinally, a decoction of bark was taken for diarrhoea, varicose veins, haemorrhoids and enteritis, and as a gargle for sore throats. Externally it was used to heal wounds and staunch bleeding. The oak gall (or oak apple) was also prescribed for haemorrhoids, as well as bleeding gums. Culpeper wrote that 'the water that is found in the hollow places in oaks, is very effectual against any foul or spreading scabs'.

In modern herbalism the bark is used to produce a bitter antiseptic that reduces inflammation and controls bleeding. It is also taken internally for the same conditions mentioned above. The bark is removed in spring from trees 10-25 years old and dried for use in decoctions and liquid extracts.

Acorns were eaten as food in times of famine and were roasted and ground to make a substitute coffee. The bark and galls are also used in tanning and dyeing.

There is such a wealth of magical lore associated with oak trees that it could take up a book to itself. Both oak wood and the acorns can be carried as amulets of protection — those acorn-shaped pulls on blinds are there to protect the house from evil and lightning strike! When gathering leaves, acorns or bark always leave an offering as the oak is the home of all manner of entities and this will guard against giving offence.

Pedunculate oak leaves

Oaks are part of the sacred triad and it is part of traditional British Old Craft to say that you come from "the Land of the Oak, the Ash and the Thorn".

Oak tress have very strong and protective auras which can be used to boost your own physical or mental strength. Approach the tree in an attitude of warmth and openness, tell it what you want and then get as close to the tree as you can. Wrap your arms around the trunk; place the flat of your palms against the bark; or sit down with your back up against the bole. You may be able to feel an exchange of energies, or that you in some way begin to merge with the tree. If the results are positive, keep this as your own special tree. And make some form of payment in return for the energies you've drawn off.

You can also use this special oak as the starting point for outdoor communication with other entities. This special 'relationship' with the tree can open doors to the spiritual and mythical lands of Otherworld. Passing between two oak trees can result in a very profound experience if you are in the right magical frame of mind, as this can take you into another realm of reality.

An incense made from oak is reputed to clear the mind and encourage the mental powers. This would be extremely useful for anyone undertaking a period of study or meditation.

Staff or Wand

A wand or staff of oak is ideally used for personal protection — especially if you are suffering the attentions of unwanted entities. Use the wand to draw a protective circle around yourself and you will be perfectly safe. A libation of mead would be appropriate.

 ear

The common pear (*pyrus communis*) is now extremely rare in the wild and is not universally accepted as being a native species. Oliver Rackham, expert on the British countryside accepts it as such "partly because of its widespread occurrence as isolated trees in remote places, which does not suggest planting."

Old single old trees are also found in relics of ancient woodland and pear charcoal has been widely reported from Neolithic sites, as well as being mentioned in medieval documents.

The wild pear can grow to a height of 50 feet and sometimes has thorny branches. The white blossom appears in early May and is visited by various different insects.

Pear wood is hard and fine-grained and on the rare occasions when it is available, it is highly prized by wood-turners and cabinet makers. It has also been used for making a wide range of musical instruments.

In the Middle Ages pears were used medicinally 'according to the differences of their tastes: for some pears are sweet, divers fat and unctuous, other sour, and most are harsh, especially wild pears'. All however, were taken to 'bind and stop the belly'. Culpeper claimed that wild pears were very effective if 'bound to green (i.e. fresh) wounds', preventing inflammation and effectively healing 'sooner ... than others' and reducing inflammation.

 It would appear that most medieval pears were hard cooking fruit and depending on the variety, were either eaten raw or cooked. They were also made into preserves, jams, puddings 'and sometimes comfits'. Perry, a cider-like drink made from pears, may have been introduced into England by the Normans.

Although the pear appears in Anglo-Saxon charters and was listed by Aelfric in his tree list, there is very little available by way of folk-lore but it is said that to dream of a pear tree is a good omen.

The British wild pear is the ancestor of the perry pear tree which was native to the three counties of Gloucester, Hereford and Worcestershire and probably introduced by the Normans. A large imposing tree, a mature perry pear has been recorded as being over 250 years old.

Staff or Wand

As pear wood was prized for its fine-grained timber, a wand would be a fine gift for a close friend but it appears to have very little, if any, magical significance and therefore it is difficult to ascribe any elemental influences to it.

Old Woodland Flowers

Wild flowers provide the woods with some of their most attractive features. Because many have adapted naturally to flower before the leaves develop in the shrub and canopy layers, they are regarded as the harbingers of spring. No doubt to our primitive ancestors this reawakening of the woodland contributed to the mystical significance of the many rites and rituals associated with spring.

An indication of an old wood is a rich variety of flowers, particularly if bluebells, snowdrops, wood anemones, primroses, yellow archangel and early purple orchids are present. Bluebells spread very slowly on heavy clay soils, so a carpet of them under trees could be the clue to old woodland.

Dog's mercury may seem to be a common woodland plant yet it is rarely found in recently planted woods— that is, woodland that has formed in the last 100 years— and so is also a good indicator of old woodland.

The presence of these particular flowers in a hedge row are all good indications that it originated as part of a wood, since these species spread very slowly and do not readily colonise hedgerows.

The Forest Layers

The efficiency of the woodland eco-system depends on how much of the sun's energy can be utilised by the green plants and converted into carbohydrate. The tallest trees of the wood, which form the 'canopy', are the first to receive the sun's rays and what grows beneath this layer depends on how much light can filter through to be tapped by other more lowly plants.

In beech woodlands there is very little, but oak and ash are relatively light shade-casters and a lush growth of plants can exist beneath them.

Immediately beneath the canopy will be tall bushes and small trees which form the second or 'shrub-layer' of the wood. Growing beneath the shrub layer is a mass of herbaceous plants which form the 'herb layer'. Many of these come into flower early in the year or have developed large flat leaves to make the most of what light is available.

The lowest layer of all is the 'ground layer' of mosses and liverworts. These remain green throughout the year and are actively growing even in winter.

Poplar

The two native poplars are the black (*populus nigra*) and the grey (*populus canescens*), although there is some argument as to whether the latter is an indigenous species. The black poplar is a fine, tall tree and, like the alder, is a lover of moisture. It may be found growing in damp meadows, keeping, if it can, close to a ditch or stream, where its long roots can stretch out to their full extent, water-seeking as they go — this being a tree of Elemental Water. These large roots can be a major threat to buildings and drainage systems when planted too close to them.

Modern management of the rivers and river banks have eliminated the poplar's natural habitat because this tree is the "last shadow of the vanished flood-plain wildwood". On the plus side, poplars have been known to regenerate by the fallen branches or trunks taking root in the mud to allow suckers to grow from the roots damaged by rivers in flood.

Even if it grows where there is no shelter, this tall giant of a tree that reaches a height of 50 to 80 feet, manages to withstand the gales of winter and requires great force to upset it. "A heavy fall of snow may cover it with a mantle of white and make it seem top-heavy, yet our experience is that it is a warrior and rarely comes to grief except through old age," wrote Percival Westell in *Trees*.

When the poplar is full grown it has a strong, massive trunk with deep furrows in the bark. There are few branches, if any, within easy reach, but those several feet above the ground are large and strong. The natural regeneration of the trees requires male and female poplars to grow in close proximity to each other but this now happens rarely in England and Wales.

The sticky, sharp-pointed yellowish buds of the red male catkins appear in winter, developing into long hanging catkins. The flowers add a touch of colour to the bare countryside for just a couple of days in early April, before the leaves begin to break. These fall to the ground before the shooting of the glossy, heart-shaped leaves and are known in some areas as the Devil's Fingers, where it is believed to be unlucky to pick them up.

The fluffy catkins on the female tree produce a white down that drifts away like fragments of cotton wool; the tree retains its flowers as these form the fruit which ripens in May. The female catkins are shorter than the males, are greenish in colour and do not droop.

The timber from the poplar is light but tough, and was used to make wooden shields because it absorbs shock and resists splintering. It was also used to line the bottom of carts and for the floors of oast houses where hops were dried, while the bark was part of the tanning process. In more modern times it provides the wood for items needing to be robust but light weight — artificial limbs, toys, wine crates, pallets and interior joinery.

Poplars are closely related to willows and the bark similarly contain salicin, which reduces inflammation and relieves pain. Medicinally it is used internally for rheumatoid arthritis, gout, fevers, lower back pain, urinary complaints, digestive and liver disorders, debility and anorexia. Externally it can be used to treat chilblains, haemorrhoids, infected wounds and sprains.

Older cures include using the juice to ease earache, while the crushed buds, mixed with honey were given as treatment for sore eyes. An ointment dating back to medieval times which including poplar buds as the main ingredient was used for reducing inflammation and bruising.

The poplar is another tree that doesn't appear in the Tree Alphabet, though the related aspen does. This is surprising because the red catkins would have drawn attention to the leafless tree in the spring. Many rural superstitions associate the poplar with the same christian mythic over-lay as the aspen and in some places it shares the same name as 'shivver-tree' because of its trembling leaves. It also shares the aspen's ability to cure agues and fever.

A Lincolnshire remedy states that a sufferer should cut off a lock of hair and wrap it around a branch of a poplar tree saying:

> *My aches and pains thou now must take,*
> *Instead of me I bid thee shake.*

He or she should then go straight home, speaking to no-one on the way, after that they will be free from ague forever. Some sources state that it is necessary to fast for twelve hours before attempting this charm.

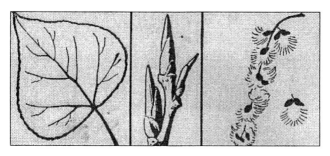

Poplar leaf, buds and female catkins

Staff or Wand

It has long been believed that poplar wood gave protection from disease and death, bringing protection and endurance. And as poplar leaves were supposed to be one of the ingredients of the witches' flying ointment, this would be an ideal wood with which to make a stang or wand. Because of the problems in obtaining a suitable piece of wood, the acquisition of such a magical tool would be a quest in itself. Make sure you leave a suitable libation or offering for such a valuable gift.

Witches' Flying Ointment

It is known how some of these flying ointments were made because a number of English and Continental writers in the 16th and 17th centuries described the methods: all the recipes contained extracts from strongly poisonous plant such as aconite, deadly nightshade and hemlock, together with cinquefoil, sweet flag, poplar leaves and parsley, mixed with soot and some sort of oil.

Rowan

The rowan (*sorbus aucuparia*) or mountain ash loves moist soil, although it can be found growing in both woods and gardens. It is common throughout the British Isles, except for the Midlands and central and southern Ireland. In Scotland, the burns and lochs, and the becks of the Lake District provide a spectacular backdrop for one of our favourite trees. It often grows singly, although in the north of Scotland there are naturally occurring pure rowan woods.

In the spring the delicate flowering branches bear a wealth of creamy-white blossoms which develop into coral-red berries in late summer. The leaves of the rowan have from eleven to nineteen 'leaflets' with tiny saw-like edges, which turn brown, red and yellow in the autumn.

Traditionally, the rowan is among the plants most positively protective against witchcraft and evil. It is reputed to have been one of the sacred trees of the Druids (because it is so often found in and around stone circles). It appears in early Scandinavian myths and its wood was used in the construction of Viking ships, to protect them from harm at sea. In Britain there was apparently no situation the rowan couldn't handle:

> *The hags came back, finding their charms*
> *Most powerfully withstood;*
> *For warlocks, witches, cannot work*
> *Where there is rowan-tree wood.*

An old Celtic name for the tree is *fid na ndruad*, or the wizard's tree, as it has a highly significant role in popular magic. *The Sacred Trees of Ireland* tells us that sprigs of rowan were "hung in the house to prevent fire-charming, used to keep the dead from walking and tied to the collar of a hound to increase his speed". The sprigs were considered to bring good luck and to protect the occupants from ill-wishing and the evil eye — hence the Celtic salutation: "Peace be here and rowan tree!"

In Lincolnshire, rowan twigs were pushed into the thatch and hayricks to stop them catching fire. Both hearths and wells might have rowan placed around them, while it was generally thought that a rowan tree near a house brought both good luck and protection; to cut it down brought misfortune.

In England the tree is either considered to be lucky or unlucky. The most often quoted superstition is that rowan crosses were used to ward of the evil intentions of witches, but in witch-lore the little rowan crosses, tied with red thread, were charms to avert negative energies from entering the house.

Rowan trees were planted near houses to protect them against spirits, especially those of the dead and in Wales, rowan trees are often found planted in churchyards to stop the dead from walking. It is obviously one of those old superstitions that has been 'borrowed' from traditional folk-lore since those of the Old Ways have no fear of the dead.

The belief in the protective powers of the rowan was obviously so strong that the church found it easier to absorb the superstition than suppress it. As a result, most of the folk-lore handed down

through the ages records the rowan as being anti-witch when in fact, in representing Elemental Fire, the rowan is one of the Nine Woods of the Beltaine Fire. It is used as an ingredient of the magical bale-fire to attract helpful spirits and other entities and for shamanic working.

In Celtic traditions it was known as the Tree of Lugh, the sun-god and was sometimes called *luisiu*, which means 'flame', possibly because of its brilliant read berries and orange leaves, which can give the appearance of fire in the autumn woodland. The rowan is also sacred to the goddess Bride, patron of poetry, blacksmiths and healing. Around Imbolc it was looked upon as the wishing tree, when red ribbons should be tied to a berry-bearing branch and the secret wish whispered to the tree.

If 'normal' folk used rowan to guard themselves against witches, witch-lore recommends that the same spells be used as protection against the Faere Folk. This is where folk-lore becomes confused because to the church and ordinary people, witch and faere was one and the same. Those rowan crosses used to protect home and live-stock, were recommended by witches to protect their goods and chattels from being stolen by the Faere Folk.

Rowan is also one of those trees which were held to cure illness and the sufferer was told to take a lock of their hair and push it into a slit in the bark; as the bark heals, so will the patient. Saxon apothecaries continued this belief by using special spoons made from rowan wood to stir their potions.

Another protective charm for the home is to tie several thin strips of rowan into a hoop that can be hung on an outside wall. This can be made into a decorative wreath to suit your personal taste.

The belief in the ability of rowan to deal with 'unquiet ghosts' also transcends all belief. Disruptive spirits and negative energies in the home can be controlled by using an infused wash or incense made from the wood and the berries. This method can be used

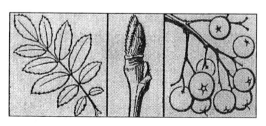

Rowan leaves, buds and berries

effectively by anyone being troubled with nightmares or disturbed sleep patterns — or hang a sprig of rowan over the bed. This does not apply to vampires, since it was a rowan stake that was driven through the heart of any undead suspected of nocturnal wanderings.

Charms bags traditionally contain a miniature stave of rowan wood for protection, together with some of the berries.

And last, but not least, the berries can be made into rowan jelly, a useful preserve that can be eaten as a jam or as an accompaniment to roast meat during the Yuletide festivities.

Staff or Wand

Rowan always works best in a personal way because it responds best if frequently handled. It is therefore the ideal wood to choose as the handle of a magical knife, or to cut for a staff or wand. It is also used instead of hazel for dowsing, while cattle herders cut their droving stick from rowan wood in the belief that it would fatten their animals. Leave some rowan jelly in thanks for your gift.

cots Pine

Apart from the yew and juniper, the Scots pine is the only native conifer of the British Isles. The true Scots pine, which once formed extensive tracts within the ancient Caledonian Forest in the Scottish Highlands, is considered to be a distinct variety (*pinus sylvestris* var. *scotia*.) Pollen records reveal that the Scots pine was the first tree to reappear when the Glacial Period ended.

Whole pine trees and pine stumps can still be found preserved under peat bogs all over Britain, mostly dating from the Boreal period, around 9,000 years ago, when climatic changes inundated the land, submerging the trees. In some places, the remains of pine stumps can be found on the foreshore, where the sea level has risen and swamped the coastal forests.

It is recognisable by its pyramidal growth which distinguishes it from the flat topped planted pines in the south. Scots pine seed has been extensively exported from Scotland during the past two or three hundred years to be planted in other parts of the country, although the native pine woods of the Caledonian Forest have been

 extensively cleared and fragmented during historic times in a similar way to the lowland oak wood.

The tree does best in peaty soil, but it thrives where there is sand, or even on a barren hillside, and it likes moisture. This is, of course an evergreen, and when the hills and woods are snow covered, the strong trunks and higher branches with their dark green leaves stand out in relief against the wintry surroundings.

Sometimes we can see a clump of several trees growing together on top of a hill; they were thought to bring good luck, and the trees' imposing silhouette against the sky line made them an attractive focal point. All over the world the Scots pine is thought of in folk-lore as a symbol of fertility, longevity (it may live for a couple of centuries or more), and good fortune. In old age the trees lose their elegant shape as the lower branches fall off and they become flat-topped and sometimes rather stricken-looking.

There is also some evidence to suggest that single pines or small clumps, may well indicate the site of a ley line and particularly a 'node' point—a place where two or more ancient trackways intersect. This appears to be especially true if the trees are located on the top of a hill.

Until the Middle Ages much of the Scottish Highlands were covered with forests of Scots pine. From the 17th century onwards deforestation took its toll and today the native pine woods of Scotland survive only as pathetic remnants. To see the trees at their best you should go to places such as Glen Affric in Inverness-shire, the Ballochbuie district of Aberdeenshire or Rothiemurchus on the north-eastern slopes of the Cairngorms. These Scottish pine forests, where pines of all ages and sizes grow amid majestic scenery of mountains and lochs, support a rich variety of wildlife.

Wordsworth extolled the virtue of the Scots pine, especially in the winter or by moonlight. And if you listen carefully beneath a cluster of pines when a gentle wind is blowing, you may hear secrets being told:

Stalwart and strong these sentry pines
Stand on the frontier line,
Guarding the gates to wonderland,
Whispering all the time.

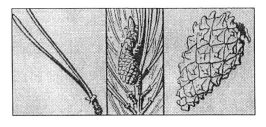

Pine cones and needles

If you would learn a simple lesson of the difference between a fir and a pine, remember that the leaves of the pine grow in pairs. They resemble two long green needles joined at the base. Search beneath a Scots pine and you should find several pairs of leaves that have fallen. These pairs of long leaves grow in circles, close together, so that the twigs look like bottle-brushes, whereas the firs have shorter, less bunchy-looking leaves.

Pine cones do *not* forecast weather as is popularly supposed. They open and close as the weather changes from dry to wet, not in advance of the change. The cones open when it is dry so that the wind-borne seeds have a chance to scatter. Were they to open during wet weather, the rain would carry the water-logged seeds straight down to the tree's roots.

Scots pine leaves, young shoots, buds, oil and tar are utilised in modern herbalism. These properties produce a bitter, aromatic, warming herb that acts as an expectorant and diuretic; improves the blood flow locally and has a tonic effect on the nerves. It is also strongly antiseptic. Pine is used internally for urinary and respiratory tract infections, and gall bladder complaints.

Externally it can be used in the treatment of arthritis, rheumatism, sciatica, poor circulation, bronchitis, catarrh, sinusitis, asthma, pneumonia, neuralgia, acne, fatigue and nervous exhaustion. The oil is used in aromatherapy for similar complaints. In addition the oil and tar are added to disinfectants, bath preparations, detergents and preparations to stimulate hair growth. It should not, however, be given to patients with allergic skin conditions.

For the Scots, the pine has a history of spiritual and inspirational significance that can be traced back to pre-christian Celtic and Pictish cultures; it is the clan totem of the Grants and the MacGregors. Recent research indicates that Scots pines were planted along the old droveways in the south of England during the 18th century as route-markers during snowy weather.

Pine is associated with the Winter Solstice and the rebirth of the sun. The cones, resin, oil and wood can be used in spells and incenses to increase fertility/virility but also as a protective element to reverse negative energies. It is also a good addition to any purification ritual.

Staff or Wand

Pine is very strongly associated with the powers of both Elemental Earth and Air and a wand or staff made from its wood can be a powerful aid when pathworking in the spiritual winter forests and with the Wild Hunt. The wood makes a sturdy protective staff to ward off all negative entities and vibrations.   A resinous wine would make an ideal libation.

trawberry Tree

Of the 40 or so species of trees that are native to Britain and Ireland, the strawberry tree (*arbutus unedo*) is one of the rarest in the wild. In Britain it no longer exists in its native state, though it is commonly planted in parks and gardens as an ornamental tree. Only in a few isolated areas in southern Ireland can the strawberry tree still be seen growing naturally.

The strawberry tree is a small evergreen, not usually more than 33 feet high. It has dark, glossy-green leaves with toothed margins, and bunches of drooping creamy-white flowers like small bells tinged with pink. As the flowers die away the previous year's fruits are finally reaching maturity. The dull reddish-brown outer layers of flaking, fibrous bark peel back to reveal the more brightly coloured inner bark which may suggest Elemental Fire.

Occasionally, the tree has a single central stem but, more often the stem divides above ground so that the plant resembles a large bush rather than a tree. Strangely enough, the tree belongs to the Heath Family (such as bilberry and ling, often called heather) but, unlike them, it will grow in chalk—though it prefers a sandy soil.

The fruits are edible, though they taste watery and insipid. The Romans found them equally unappetising, a fact referred to

in the plant's Latin name – *arbutus unedo*. The word 'unedo' is a contraction of *unum edo*, which is Latin for 'I eat one'. As the Roman naturalist Pliny explained in the first century AD, "The fruit is held in no esteem, the reason for its name being that a person will only eat one."

In some European countries around

the Mediterranean, however, the fruits are made into a delicious liqueur.

Two hundred years ago the strawberry tree was much more plentiful, but large scale felling for charcoal has taken its toll. The best place to see the tree in its natural habitat is around the lakes of Killarney where it can be seen growing on cliffs and rocky slopes. Here the trees have reached a considerable age. The tree regenerates itself by putting out new shoots from the fallen main stem; as a result it is extremely difficult to arrive at a precise age for any individual tree.

There is little folk-lore associated with the strawberry tree, although it is the first of the seven Shrub Trees (less important than the seven Chieftain Trees and seven Peasant Trees) of medieval Celtic lore where it was called *caithnei* in Old Irish. Its leaves and flowers were believed to be an antidote to poison and plague in the 17th century.

Staff or Wand
Because of the rarity of the wild strawberry tree anyone attempting to cut wood for a wand or staff deserves to be strung up from it!

Leaf, buds and fruits

The Wildwood

Historically, the term 'wildwood' is the name given to the forests as they were some 6,000 years ago, before human interference. The pollen records for that time confirm that elms made up a substantial component of the wildwood, along with oak, birch and lime.

On a magical level, the Wild Wood refers to those strange, eerie places that remain the realm of Nature and untamed by man. It is the Otherworld of unearthly and potentially dangerous beings. This is the realm of Pan and the Wild Hunt. In modern psychology it refers to the dark inner recesses of the mind, the wild and tangled growths of the unconscious.

Here, among the trees, we are never sure that what we see is reality or illusion and the nearest most of us come to experiencing it is through that wonderful passage in *The Wind in the Willows* where Mole is lost ...

"... he penetrated to where the light was less, and trees crouched nearer and nearer ... Everything was very still now. The dusk advanced on him steadily, rapidly, gathering in behind and before; and the light seemed to be draining away like flood-water ... Then the whistling began ..."

Meriem Clay-Egerton wrote extensively on the subject of trees and produced some extremely evocative pieces relating to

Wild Wood experiences which were, sadly, left unpublished at the time of her death.   Here she describes the strange half-light that anyone who walks in the Wild Wood will immediately recognise.

"I was always glad to go deeper into the apparent gloom because I would be beyond one of the woodland's outer barriers ...

"... To me this was a place that had obviously been held as a sacred area for so very long now that it had in its turn breathed this very atmosphere itself and so projected this onto a mind which was prepared or conditioned to be both sympathetic and empathetic to various woodlands and their forms of existence ... it resembled what I might envisage as a naturally constructed 'cathedral'. Here lived and breathed holiness and beauty ..."

It is impossible to describe the sensations of the Wild Wood, but no one who has walked there can remain unchanged by the experience.

Whitebeam

The whitebeam (*sorbus aria*) gets its name from the white under-side of the leaves which comes from their coat of felty hairs which help to check water loss—a useful feature on the dry lime-stone soils on which the tree often grows.   In the wild, the white-beam is found chiefly on the chalk of central, south and south-eastern England. Its main strongholds are the Chilterns, where it can be found in scrub thickets, open woods, clearings and along hedgerows, and the steep slopes of the South Downs.

In May or June the tree displays an impressive coating of white, five-petalled flowers that are clustered in loose bunches. By October the berries have ripened to a rich shiny scarlet that hang heavily on the twigs. Although not poisonous to man, the berries are not very palatable, so can be left to the squirrels, hedgehogs and voles.

Despite the fact that it is recognised as one of our native trees, it does not appear to feature in British folk-lore. According to the entry in *Trees in the Wild*, little is known about its postglacial history because it grows in chalk and, unlike peat, chalk does not

preserve pollen records.. It is a common sight throughout southern England and less frequently at scattered sites in northern England and Scotland. In Ireland the same species can be found in Galway, but rarely anywhere else.. Some authorities have raised the doubt as to whether the whitebeam is a native tree as there are other species that are much more widespread.

Staff or Wand

The wood is hard and pale yellow and suitable to be cut for a staff or wand. From the way this tree shimmers from green to silver as the leaves turn with the wind, it suggests an association with Elemental Air.

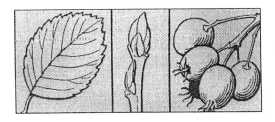

Leaf, buds and berries

ROOT & BRANCH

An extract from Henry Wadsworth Longfellow's

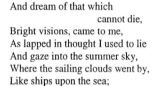

Prelude

Pleasant it was, when woods were
         green,
And winds were soft and low,
To lie amid some sylvan scene,
Where, the long drooping boughs
         between.
Shadows dark and sunlight sheen
Alternate come and go;

Or where the denser grove receives
No sunlight from above,
But the dark foliage interweaves
In one unbroken roof of leaves,
Underneath whose sloping eaves
The shadows hardly move.

Beneath some patriarchal tree
I lay upon the ground;
His hoary arms uplifted he,
And all the broad leaves over me
Clapped their little hands in glee,
With one continuous sound;-

A slumberous sound, a sound that
         brings
The feelings of a dream,
As of innumerable wings,
As, when a bell no longer swings,
Faint the hollow murmur rings
O'er meadow, lake and stream.

And dream of that which
         cannot die,
Bright visions, came to me,
As lapped in thought I used to lie
And gaze into the summer sky,
Where the sailing clouds went by,
Like ships upon the sea;

Dreams that the soul of youth
         engage
Ere Fancy has been quelled;
Old legends of the monkish page,
Traditions of the saint and sage,
Tales that have the rime of age.
And chronicles of Eld.

And, loving still these quaint old
         themes,
Even in the city's throng
I feel the freshness of the streams,
That, crossed by shades and sunny
        gleams,
Water the green land of dreams,
The holy land of song.

Therefore, at Pentecost, which
        brings,
The Spring, clothed like a bride,
When nestling buds unfold their
        wings,
And bishop's-caps have golden
        rings,
Musing upon many things
I sought the woodlands wide

The green trees whispered low and
                              mild:
It was a sound of joy!
They were my playmates when a child,
And rocked me in their arms so wild:
Still they looked at me and smiled,
As if I were a boy;

And ever whispered, mild and low,
'Come, be a child once more!'
And waved their long arms to and fro
And beckoned solemnly and slow:
O, I could not choose but go
Into the woodlands hoar, -

Into the blithe and breathing air,
Into the solemn wood,
Solemn and silent everywhere!
Nature with folded hands seemed there,
Kneeling at her evening prayer!
Like one in prayer I stood

Before me rose an avenue
Of tall and sombrous pines;
Abroad their fan-like branches grew,
And, where the sunshine darted
                              through,
Spread a vapour soft and blue,
In long and sloping lines.

And, falling on my weary brain,
Like a fast-falling shower,
The dreams of youth came back again,
Low lispings of the summer rain,
As once upon the flower ...

Wild Service Tree

In England, the wild service tree (*sorbus torminalis*) is regarded as an indicator of ancient woodland although there is little written about it in books on the subject. It is a small to medium sized tree with a wide crown. The leaves of the wild service tree are unlike those of any other members of the *sorbus* family (like hawthorn and rowan) and for this reason, the tree can easily be mistaken for a maple. It is a colourful tree in autumn when it is covered with small brown berries.

There is, what is known as the 'bastard service tree' which is fairly common in city streets and parks. This is a cross between the rowan and the service tree of Fontainbleau, itself a hybrid of whitebeam and wild service tree.

There is brief mention of the wild service tree in the herbals where the berries are said to have health-giving properties and a cure for colic, while an infusion made from the flower-stalks and leaves 'is incomparable for consumptive bodies and cures the green-sickness of virgins'.

Apart from that, there is no apparent mention of the tree in folk-lore or in any of the usual texts governing tree-lore. Because the tree is related to the *sorbus* family, which also includes hawthorn and rowan, it is reasonable to assume that

Maple-like leaves of the wild service tree

Berries of the wild service tree

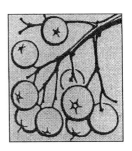

similar magical propensities can be associated with the leaves and berries.

The fact that the tree is of ancient lineage and infrequently included in later tree-lore, also suggests that it was another important Faere tree. Like the alder, it was probably a sacred tree to the indigenous people of Britain.

Staff or Wand

The wood is fine-grained and valuable. Having been used for pistol and gun-stocks in the past, it could rightly claim to represent Elemental Fire like the hawthorn and rowan. A wand made from wild service wood should be highly prized and not given or received lightly.

The Nine Sacred Woods
for the Need-fire
Ash

Birch

Yew

Hazel

Rowan,

Willow

Pine

Thorn

and all other trees mentioned as being
traditionally sacred with the exception
of the oak and the elder

In medieval Ireland, under Brehon Law trees
were divided into four categories with a scale
of fines for their unlawful felling

The Seven Irish Chieftain Trees
Oak-dair

Hazel-coll

Holly-cuileann

Yew-ibur

Ash-iundius

Pine-ochtach

Apple-aball

Seven Peasant Trees
Alder-fernn
Willow-sail
Hawthorn-sceith
Rowan-caerthann
Birch-beithe
Elm-leam
? - idha

Seven Shrub Trees
Blackthorn-draidean
Elder-tron
White hazel-fincoll
White poplar-crithach
Arbutus-caithne
? - feorus
? - crann-fir

Eight Bramble Trees
Fern-raith
Bog-myrtle-rait
Furze-aiteand
Briar-dris
Heath-fraech
Ivy-eideand
Broom-gilcoch
Gooseberry-spin

Willow

There are five native species of willow although the aromatic Bay willow (*salix pentandra*) is rarely found these days in the wild. Also called Black Willow or Sweet Willow.

Crack willow (*salix fragilis*), of *Wind in the Willows* fame, are usually seen as gaunt, pollarded trees, hock-deep in water, their naked branches reaching skywards like antlers.

Goat willow (*salix caprea*) or Pussy Willow, whose catkins provide a veritable banquet for brimstone butterflies and bees in March, when there is little other forage for them. Also known as Sally or Palm Willow.

Grey willow (*salix cinerea*) or Sallow grows on fens and marshes, in damp woods and by streams and ponds as a shrub or small tree. Also referred to as Pussy Willow in some areas.

White willow (*salix alba*) or Cricket-bat Willow is a native of river and marsh, having silver felted leaves which stream dramatically in the wind.

Sallow or grey willow

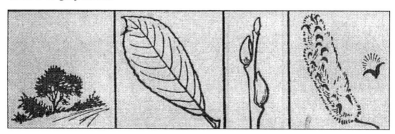

The earliest record of willow's use by man was in Neolithic times when causeways of willow branches were laid across boggy ground to provide a safe path. By medieval times, in addition to making baskets, fish-traps, fences and coracles, willow was used in tanning, as fodder, to attract bees, to make artists' charcoal, to produce purple dye, and to prevent erosion along the banks of rivers and ditches. The downy covering of the seeds was used as mattress stuffing.

Later, in days when every lowland English village had its basket maker and its 'withy' beds, Richard Jefferies wrote: "An advantage of willow is that it enables the farmer to derive a profit from land that would otherwise be comparatively valueless, to provide arable farms with market baskets, chaff baskets, bassinets and hampers. This willow harvest is looked forward to by the cottagers who live along the rivers as an opportunity for earning extra money." (*Country Illustrated* vol. 4. No. 47). Today the willow is popularly used to make bio-degradable coffins for woodlands burials.

All willows belong to the large family of *Salix*, which has between 350 and 500 species, depending on the source you consult. This confusion arises because hybrids occur together with parent species and because the willows themselves are variable.

In the lowlands all over the British Isles, willows are the most characteristic tree in the landscape, lining the banks of rivers large and small, from the Thames to the Shannon.

White willow

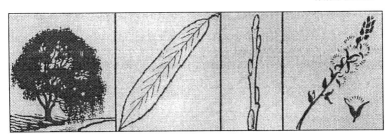

Medicinally, the bark of the white willow was used to alleviate pain, relieve headaches, and reduce fevers. It was also used for rheumatism, arthritis, internal bleeding, inflammations, gout, heartburn, colds, nervous insomnia, digestive problems and stomach complains. Externally, it was applied for burns, sores, cuts and skin rashes. Culpeper wrote: "The leaves are bruised and boiled in wine, and drank, stays the heat of lust in man or woman, and quite distinguishes it, if it be long used."

In modern herbalism, the bark of the white willow is collected from young branches during the growth period. Willow is anti-inflammatory, analgesic, antipyretic, antirheumatic and astringent. Interestingly, some of willow's active constituents, while sharing the pain-relieving effects of asprin, have a more sustained action in the body and fewer side effects.

Willow bark helps to reduce high fevers and to relieve the pain of arthritis and headaches. Although these claims have not been proved clinically, the indications are strongly supported by the fact that the bark was used in a similar way to asprin long before the invention of the drug.

In folk-lore the willow was associated with sorrow and lost love. Sprigs were sometimes worn as a sign of mourning; or by those who had been forsaken in love, hence the words of the old folk-song: "*All around my hat I will wear the green willow*".

The willow is listed in the Celtic Tree Alphabet and is referred to as one of the Peasant Trees, bearing the name *saille.* In Celtic times, groves of willow were frequented by those who wished to learn eloquence, or be granted visions, prophetic dreams or inspirations.

Because of the willow's association with rivers, it is representative of Elemental Water. It is usually the bark of the tree that is used magically in incense but a bundle of twigs can also be used to concentrate Elemental Fire. The twigs should be lit from a special fire or consecrated candle and then plunged into consecrated water. This is known as a 'fire potion' and can be used for magical cleansing. To increase the potency, add an infusion of the appropriate herb. The potion may be drunk or applied as a compress of cotton wool to increase psychic powers. This is the poor witch's answer to the blacksmith's 'thunder water'.

Staff or Wand

Willow is one of the woods from which to make the traditional magic wand. This should be cut from the tree with a single blow, having first asked the tree for its permission and made a suitable offering. Shamen, sorcerers and enchanters were all said to favour wands made of willow because it can be used to command the spirits of the dead.

These magical associations were obviously well known as existing folk-lore claims that using a willow staff to herd animals is guaranteed to drive them to the 'devil'. Using a willow wand to renounce your baptism was said to guarantee that the devil will grant you supernatural powers. These are, no doubt, throw-backs to pre-christian times when willow was acknowledged as being the 'badge' of the cunning man or woman.

Wych Elm

Not too long ago, many people would have considered the English or common elm (*ulmus procera*) to epitomise the English countryside. Immortalised by Constable in his painting of *The Cornfield*, this stately tree has been decimated by Dutch elm disease and the smaller wych elm (*ulmus glabra*) is now more widespread.

Elm had reached southern England by 9,500 years ago, spreading west to Wales and eastern Ireland: it reached northern Scotland by 6,200. There was a dramatic decline between 5,500 and 5,000 ago which some authorities believe to be caused by Dutch elm disease, although the trees did recover.

The wych elm is a native tree occurring in woods and beside streams mainly in the west and north of Britain, especially in hilly districts. Historically, elms were coppiced and pollarded and in some counties, enormous old pollards can still be seen. There is, however, considerable disagreement about the classifications and some claim that both the wych and the common elm are native species. Certainly it is the common elm that appears in the medieval herbals.

Wych elm

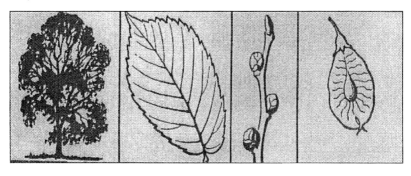

The wych can be also distinguished from the common elm by a number of characteristics. Wych elms are not as tall and grow in irregular shapes up to 100 feet. The lower branches start to arch from nearer the base of the trunk, while the upper branches appear twisted. The dull grey or blackish bark is smooth when young but turns brownish-grey, fissured and ribbed in mature specimens.

On the wych elm, the dense clusters of reddish-brown flowers appear in March and April before the leaves, and note that the wych elm's flat fruit has the one seed in the centre of the fruit, not above the centre, as in the common elm. The flowers are brightly coloured with crimson or purple anthers and white filaments. The leaves are bright green; rough above and downy and rough on the underside.

Oliver Rackham writing in his *History of the Country-side*, devoted a whole chapter to the tree and observed that elms are "the most complex and difficult trees in western Europe, and the most intimately linked to human affairs".

Traces have been found to record that early Neolithic sites showed evidence of elm wood being used for all manner of purposes. Giraldus Cambrensis wrote in the 12th century that the Welsh longbow was made of elm, instead of yew as in England. The timber had many domestic uses including coffin making. Elm was one of the timbers used for water-pipes, and excavations have revealed surviving stretches of old mains during modern building work. Elm piles were laid under bridges and buildings, including under old Waterloo Bridge and today, when available is still used in boat-building.

With all these water association it would be logical to assume that the elm represented Elemental Water but, in fact, it is aligned with Elemental Earth. Considering another name for the tree is *elven,* perhaps it should not surprise us that the elm is a tree of the Faere Folk and that anyone taking the wood should leave offerings of wine or mead, or small silver coins for them.

ROOT & BRANCH

In medieval times the leaves of the elm were used in ointment for burns, wounds and haemorrhoids, and in a decoction for skin inflammations, while sap from the branches was reputed to cure baldness.

Culpeper wrote: "The leaves or the bark used with vinegar, cure scurf and leprosy very effectively: the decoction of the leaves, bark and root, being bathed, heals broken bones". The inner bark of slippery elm, or red elm (*ulmus rubra*) was used as a laxative and, as a convalescent drink, to soothe sore throats and intestinal upsets.

In modern herbalism, the common elm may be used in lotions for skin complaints but is no longer of major importance since the demise of most English elms from Dutch elm disease. Wych elm or as it is called in southern England wych-hazel is also used in a lotion or ointment which is particularly effective against burns.

Most modern preparations come from the slippery elm, whose inner bark is stripped from the trunks and larger branches in spring, dried and powdered for use in decoctions, liquid extracts, ointments, poultices, powders and tablets.

Medicinally, it is used internally for gastric and duodenal ulcers, gastris, colitis and digestive problems in infants. Externally for sore throat, coughs, wounds, burns, boils, abscesses and chilblains. It is often added as a soothing element to cough mixture.

English, or common elm

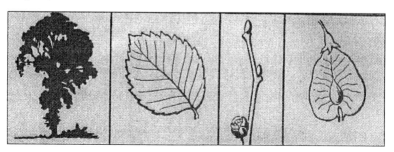

Elm was one of the plants chosen by Dr Edward Bach for his flower essence remedies for inspiration. The remedy is made by infusing the flowers of slippery elm in the sunlight for four hours. The dose is four drops, four times a day, under the tongue. Because the bark contains a trace mineral valuable to the brain stem, a tincture of slippery elm has been found useful in treating depression.

Because of its associations with Elven or Faere Folk, the site of an elm is thought to be a gateway to Otherworld. Incense made from the wood can be used to encourage inspiration and boost confidence. Tiny pieces placed in a pouch will give the wearer the gift of eloquence.

Staff or Wand
Should you be fortunate enough to acquire sufficient elm to make a wand or staff, this can be used in magical workings to gain inspiration and insight — but beware of its Faere powers!

e w

Last, but certainly not least, the common yew (*taxus baccata*) must be the most fascinating and mysterious, if not oldest, of all our native trees. The yew is said to be the longest-lived tree in Britain, some having lived for more than 1,000 years. Yew trees are usually solitary but the best place to see them is the famous yew wood at Kingley Vale, near Chichester which is regarded as the finest in Europe.

The yew likes limy soil and there is an island on Loch Lomond that was once covered with them, from which bows were supplied, for its hard flexible wood was the best for the purpose. The English longbow was made of yew and some of the oldest weapons that archaeologists have discovered are made from yew and date from the Palaeolithic times—about 250,000 years ago! A yew spear found in Essex was estimated to be some 150,000 years old.

This is a dark, brooding, evergreen tree which reaches a height of fifteen to fifty feet; the trunk is massive because of the numerous shoots joining together. The shade beneath a large yew is

extremely dense, which means that not enough sunlight filters through to allow any green plants to grow. Although Percival Westell thought it: "A beautiful tree in winter or early spring, when small scarlet fairy lamps hang about its dark green cloak."

The long flat leaves are poisonous and so are the

Flower spray of yew

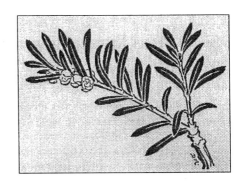

seeds and bark — the crushed seeds were once used as an arrow poison. The small male flowers appear in clusters but the female flowers are solitary. These develop into a hard olive-green seed inside a red fleshy cup which the birds enjoy as they are sweet and full of syrup.

Pliny wrote that the tree was "so toxic that even wine-flasks for travellers made of its wood in Gaul are known to have caused death". While Gerard claimed that the English yew was not poisonous, he wrote: "In most countries, it hath such a malign quality, that it is not safe to sleep, or long to rest under the shadow thereof".

In medieval medicine yew was used as a purgative, and to treat heart and liver diseases, gout, rheuatism, arthritis and urinary infections. Culpeper wrote "though it is sometimes given usefully in obstructions of the liver and billious complaints, those experiments seem too few to recommend it to be used without the greatest caution".

Smoke from the burning leaves was supposed to repel gnats and mosquitoes, as well as rats and mice.

Despite being highly poisonous, the yew has always been surrounded by legend and is a symbol of immortality. Many of our ancient yews are to be found in churchyards and if they are well over a thousand years then they are more than likely mark-

ing pagan sites of worship.   With the arrival of christianity, these were taken over and churches were built to obliterate the pagan sacred sites.   Before the advent of christianity, the yew was looked upon as a sacred tree and a symbol of everlasting life; after that time the tree was denigrated to mean something sinister or dangerous. To bring cuttings of yew into the home was said to lead to death in the family.

Many ancient yews are found growing on what are known to be ancient burial sites dating from Neolithic, Celtic and Saxon periods.   Studies concerning the alignment of church buildings in relation to ancient yews has suggested that this indicates the age of the sites and gives a minimum age for the trees. Where the church is west or east of the yew, the site is Celtic; where north or north-east of it, Saxon; and where south of the yew, Neolithic. The yew is one of the Celtic Chieftain Trees, out of which were carved warriors' breast plates, dagger handles, and the sacred brooch worn by the kings or Ireland to be passed on to his successor.

Yew leaves can be used in pouches and incense to contact the Mighty Dead and the incense smoke is a perfect aid to divination, or answers to questions that can be sought by scrying or the pendulum. Because yew is representative of Elemental Earth, it can aid communicate with earth elementals, particularly those that safeguard treasures — material and magical. Warning: Incense containing yew should only be used outside or in a well ventilated room as inhaling too much may be dangerous

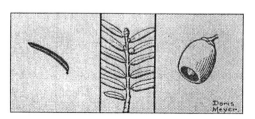

Leaves and berries

Staff or Wand

A staff or wand of yew should be treated with great care as it acts as a bridge between the worlds. Because it is the tree of weaponry it has a martial aura to it and very often the only payment for taking yew wood is blood. A pin-prick will be sufficient and it is a price worth paying.

Rods or staffs of yew are associated in legend with many magical powers and used as a dowsing rod, the yew can lead the bearer to recover missing treasure or property. In Gaelic legend, the 'white wand' was a special tool cut from yew which gave the bearer incredible magic powers, being associated with the 'spell of knowledge' - a magical working to give the enquirer access to Otherworld and the realms of Faere. Unfortunately, this could also lead to the death of the enquirer.

The Scots believed that a man could denounce an enemy while holding a yew wand and prove his case because those hearing his complaint would be able to see he was telling the truth.

With its Otherworld connections, yew was also a protector of the spirits of the dead and carved yew wands were often placed in the coffins of country burials — this later became a belief that it would prevent the dead from walking.

ummary

The majority of other trees now growing in the British Isles were those introduced by man because of their practical use or purely for their beauty. The Romans brought the edible chestnut and walnut trees. In later years the Norway spruce, cedar or Lebanon, horse chestnut and sycamore became naturalised.

Additional species of trees wasn't all that the Romans brought with them. They also introduced the formal calendar. At that time, the Celts occupying most of the British Isles had only two seasons: summer and winter — a calculation still reflected in the altering of the clocks to comply with British Summer Time. Their livestock was taken out to pasture at the beginning of summer and brought back in to their winter shelter as the season grew colder.

These seasons, the books tell us quite categorically, fell on 1st May and 31st October respectively but this fails to observe that the original Julian calendar (augmented in 45BC) was soon out of alignment, having to be modified several times before the Gregorian calendar was introduced in 1582. This resulted in a further 10 days being removed completely. These changes meant there was a lot of political 'put-and-take' in agreeing what should be moved and what should be left out but what has not been taken into account is the naturally occurring phenomena of *precession*.

The sun and moon exert a gravitational pull on the earth's equatorial bulge, causing the planet to 'wobble' in a very slow cycle now known as precession. This is a slow, almost circular motion, which returns to the same place every 26,000 years. In the history of man, precession has produced some strange anomalies, often bringing about some drastic changes in seasonal calculations which is confirmed by historians and archaeologists who make it their business to study such things.

We also know that weather conditions have changed drastically over the past five hundred years and that the only things that remain constant are the solstices and equinoxes – and the steady, relentless tramp of Nature. Calendars offers a sense of purpose and identity - a feeling of belonging but how useful are they to the outcome of magical working? The answer is: not very if the calendar fails to synchronise with *natural* tides and energies.

There are now eight main festivals in the Witch's year—but what if there are really only four? Vernal Equinox; Summer Solstice; Autumnal Equinox and Winter Solstice. What if precession has caused the civil and astronomical calendars to move out of alignment as it has with other cultures whose history dates back 6,000 years? It makes far more sense if the Celts celebrated Beltaine at Spring Equinox; Lughnasad (the feast of Lugh, the sun-god) at Summer Solstice; harvest and the year's end at Autumnal Equinox and Imbolc at Winter Solstice.

As George Ewart Evens pointed out about country folk in *The Pattern under the Plough:* "Many of them cherished beliefs – beliefs, moreover that they acted upon – dating from a period well before the coming of Christianity ... surviving into the 20th century, unobtrusive yet resilient in a rural underground that, during the time the old traditional society flourished, was rarely suspected much less disclosed." They worked according to the seasons and not by any church or civil calendar.

Neither does Nature work by any set calendar, which means that it isn't always possible to celebrate 'bringing in the may' on the 31st April if Nature decrees that the blossom will not appear until the second or third week of May! The two main agricultures festivals were held in the spring and at the end of the harvest; and it is significant that they have always been associated with Witches whose chief celebratory rites they were – but it is doubtful whether these, too, were governed by the civil calendar.

Country people and true Witches still synchronise their workings by Nature's own way of telling the seasons – by reading the signs of the trees as our British ancestors have done for 7,000 years.

ources

13 Moons, Fiona Walker-Craven (ignotus)
777, Aleister Crowley (Weiser)
Ancient Woodland, O Rackham (Arnold)
Brother Cadfael's Herb Garden, Talbot & Whiteman (LittleBrown)
Country Seasons, Philip Cloucas (Windward)
Culpepper's Complete Herbal, N. Culpepper (Foulsham)
Dictionary of Omens & Superstitions , Philippa Waring (Souvenir)
Encyclopaedia of Herbs & Their Uses, Deni Brown, (RHS)
The Englishman's Flora, Geoffrey Grigson (Phoenix)
The Ever-changing Woodlands, (Reader's Digest)
The Evergreen World, (Reader's Digest)
Hedgerow, Thomas & White (Ash & Grant)
Man, Myth & Magic (Marshall Cavendish)
Natural History of the British Isles, Pat Morris (CLB)
Nature's Medicine Chest (Reader's Digest)
The Patchwork Landscape (Reader's Digest)
The Tree Book, J Edward Milner (Channel 4)
Trees In The Wild, Gerald Wilkinson (Hope)
Superstitions of the Countryside, E & M A Radford (Arrow)
Tree Medicine, Tree Magic, Ellen Evert Hopman (Phoenix)
Trees, Westell & Harvey (Macmillan)
Trees of Britain & Europe, Press and Hosking (New Holland)
The White Goddess, Robert Graves (Faber & Faber)
Witchcraft—A Tradition Renewed, Evan John Jones (Hale)
A Witch's Countryside Treasury, Harriss and Draco (ignotus)

Index

Hearth & Garden

Gabrielle Sidonie has been more than
generous in sharing
remembrances of times past, using
family recipes and household hints that have
been handed down from generation to
generation, some still existing in the form of
treasured journals and notebooks.

The Witch's Treasury for Hearth & Garden
certainly fulfils its
intended purpose – to preserve old
traditional methods by adapting them for
use in today's home and garden.

ISBN: 1 903768 06 3 : paperback : £9.95
from ignotus press

Countryside

Mélusine Draco and Paul Harriss's,
Witch's Treasury of the Countryside
is for those who would like to understand
more about the countryside from both the
countryman's and the wise woman's (or
cunning man's) perspective. As a place to
be respected and not interfered with
because of an overall ignorance of
country ways. The witch is a natural part
of the countryside and her magic, like
Nature, is often red in tooth and claw.
Hopefully this book will encourage a new
generation of witches to have the courage
to follow the age–old observances (in spirit
if not in practice) and help return power to
the *genius loci* of the land.

ISBN: 1 903768 08 X : paperback : £9.95
from ignotus press

ignotus press